MW00981703

AMSTERDAM

MICHAEL'S GUIDE SERIES INCLUDES:

MICHAEL'S GUIDE ARGENTINA, CHILE, PARAGUAY
                    & URUGUAY
MICHAEL'S GUIDE BOLIVIA & PERU
MICHAEL'S GUIDE ECUADOR, COLOMBIA & VENEZUELA
MICHAEL'S GUIDE BRAZIL
MICHAEL'S GUIDE SOUTH AMERICA (Continental)

MICHAEL'S GUIDE NORTHERN CALIFORNIA
MICHAEL'S GUIDE SOUTHERN CALIFORNIA
MICHAEL'S GUIDE CALIFORNIA

MICHAEL'S GUIDE SCANDINAVIA
MICHAEL'S GUIDE SCOTLAND
MICHAEL'S GUIDE SWITZERLAND
MICHAEL'S GUIDE HUNGARY
MICHAEL'S GUIDE TURKEY

MICHAEL'S GUIDE NEW YORK CITY
MICHAEL'S GUIDE LONDON
MICHAEL'S GUIDE PARIS
MICHAEL'S GUIDE AMSTERDAM
MICHAEL'S GUIDE BRUSSELS & ANTWERP
MICHAEL'S GUIDE FRANKFURT
MICHAEL'S GUIDE ROME
MICHAEL'S GUIDE MADRID
MICHAEL'S GUIDE BARCELONA
MICHAEL'S GUIDE JERUSALEM

AMSTERDAM

Series editor:
Michael Shichor

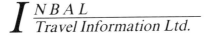

Inbal Travel Information Ltd.
P.O.Box 39090 Tel Aviv Israel 61390

Intl. ISBN 965-288-066-3

Distributed in the United Kingdom by:
Kuperard (London) Ltd.
9, Hampstead West
224 Iverson Road
West Hampstead
London NW6 2HL

U.K. ISBN 1-870668-40-5

CONTENTS

*T*ABLE OF MAPS

Preface

Amsterdam is one of Europe's commercial and cultural capitals. Its citizens are outgoing and independent; they speak many languages fluently, and visitors will find them exceptionally friendly and helpful. The tradition of claiming land from the sea since the 17th century seems to epitomize the practical and enterprising character of the Dutch. Amsterdam also has a well-established tradition of tolerance, dating back to the 16th century when many Protestants sought refuge here. Amsterdam also absorbed Jews who fled from the Inquisition, and in more recent years many immigrants have settled here — from Surinam, Britain, Germany, Spain, Morocco, Yugoslavia and other places. Since the 1960s, Amsterdam has been a center for young people exploring Europe and seeking alternative lifestyles. This mixture of people adds to the vibrant and dynamic atmosphere here.

Amsterdam has a university with 30,000 students, a well-known and highly reputed Philharmonic Orchestra and National Ballet, as well as academies for architecture, nuclear physics, design, film and the performing arts.

The traditional attractions of Amsterdam continue to charm visitors — narrow houses tilting at crazy angles over peaceful canals, gablestones each telling a different story, and wonderful art museums. Modern Amsterdammers preserve their heritage, but are always moving forward, exploring something new. The open, tolerant attitude of the city will surprise many, when they are offered a marijuana menu in a coffee shop or when they pass through the red-light district.

To compile this Guide, our researchers spent months exploring the museums and historic sites, discovering exciting corners of the city, and investigating every neighborhood. They sampled the fascinating cuisine in a wide range of restaurants, and visited jazz clubs, bars and coffee shops, in order to make up-to-the-minute recommendations. The staff at Inbal compiled and edited the Guide.

We hope to introduce you to the many facets of this charming and dynamic city, and to put before you the opportunities which it offers. Our aim is to give you a deeper understanding of Amsterdam, to lead you to its best and most exciting attractions, and to ensure that you derive maximum pleasure from your trip. We are sure that the effort invested in compiling this Guide will be justified by your enhanced enjoyment.

Michael Shichor

Using this Guide

In order to reap maximum benefit from the information concentrated in this Guide, we advise the traveler to carefully read the following advice and to act upon it. The facts contained in this book are meant to help the tourist find his or her way around, and to assure that he sees the most, with maximum savings of money, time and effort.

The information contained in the Introduction should be read in its entirety as it will supply you with details which will help in making the early decisions and arrangements for your trip. Reviewing the material thoroughly, and acting upon it, means that you will be more organized and set for your visit. Upon arrival, you will already feel familiar and comfortable with Amsterdam, more so than would otherwise have been the case.

The basic guideline in all 'MICHAEL'S GUIDE' publications is to survey places in a primarily geographical sequence. The detailed introductory chapters discuss general topics and specific aspects of getting organized. The tour routes, laid out geographically, lead the visitor up and down the city's streets, providing a survey of the sights and calling attention to all those details which deepen one's familiarity with Amsterdam, and make a visit there so much more enjoyable.

Following the tour routes, we have included a selection of 'Excursions', which are all extremely interesting and worth a visit. Each of these excursions makes for a very pleasant day trip out of Amsterdam.

A concise list of 'Musts' follows, describing those sights without which a visit to Amsterdam is not complete.

The numerous maps which accompany the tour routes have been specially prepared, and show the visitor exactly how to reach the sights and attractions discussed in the tour routes. The maps will make your exploration of Amsterdam more efficient and pleasurable.

Since Amsterdam is a magnet for lovers of gourmet cuisine, fine shopping and entertainment, we have devoted special chapters to 'Making the Most of Your Stay' in the city. Here you will find a broad range of possibilities to suit your budget, which will help you enjoy your stay.

To further facilitate use of this Guide, we have included a detailed index at the back of the book, which lists all the major sights, and refers you to the place where each sight is discussed in greatest detail.

Because times change, and cities are dynamic, an important rule of thumb when traveling, especially to a vibrant city like Amsterdam, should be to consult local sources of information. Although we have made every effort to confirm that facts are up-to-date, changes do occur and travelers may find certain facts somewhat inaccurate when arriving at their destinations, and for this we apologize in advance.

In order to be as up-to-date as possible, cooperation and assistance are necessary from those of you who have enjoyed the information contained in this Guide. For this purpose we have included a short questionnaire at the end of the Guide, and will be most grateful to those who complete it and send it to us. A **complimentary copy** of the new edition will be forwarded to those of you who take the time, and whose contribution will appear in the up-dated version.

During your visit you will see and experience many things — we have therefore left several blank pages at the back of the Guide. These are for you, to jot down those special experiences of people and places, feelings and significant happenings along the way.

Have a pleasant and exciting trip — Bon Voyage!

*I*NTRODUCTION

Part One — A First Taste of What's to Come

Amsterdam, an unending circus of street performers and musicians, a parade of faces from around the world, dozens of languages, and restaurants serving food from as many places, nightlife that buzzes till dawn, and a wealth of art museums and historical buildings.

Like half of the Netherlands, Amsterdam was wrested from sea and swampland, and only exists thanks to continuing efforts to fight back the sea. The basic layout of the city dates back 400 years to the Golden Age of Amsterdam. Historical buildings are carefully preserved, and tree-lined canals create a soothing peaceful ambience.

Amsterdam is a welcoming city, accepting persecuted minorities, open and tolerant to all religions and lifestyles, yet with a strong sense of tradition.

Here there is freedom of speech and religion, and an easygoing, permissive attitude. The availability of drugs is something you will notice almost as soon as you notice that half the population seems to get around by bicycle. Drug abuse and prostitution are not unique to Amsterdam, but the city confronts such problems in bold and experimental ways.

Perhaps this, above all, is what makes the city unique — the balance of maximum personal freedom within a social, ethical framework; a readiness to find imaginative solutions to practical problems.

History

The philosopher Alfred North Whitehead called the 17th century the 'century of genius', and it seems that much of that genius emanated from the tiny Republic of the Netherlands and, more specifically, from its center, Amsterdam. The canals, the quaint houses, the monuments, and most of what the tourist sees in this lovely city date back to Amsterdam's Golden Age, in the first half of the 17th century. Amsterdam became the richest city in

_I_NTRODUCTION

the world, with the richest men in the world. The Netherlands acquired colonies in five continents and competed successfully with the national powers of Europe. Its fleets controlled crucial sea lanes, and its merchants regulated world markets. Luxury goods flowed through Amsterdam, and hundreds of ships crowded her harbor. Together with material growth, rose a tolerance towards religious minorities which was unique in Europe. In the liberal climate, scientific experimentation and the development of new philosophies thrived. Dutch art produced a pantheon of masters such as Vermeer, Frans Hals and Rembrandt, who influenced the course of Western art.

These great achievements are particularly significant coming from a tiny land, a bleak, sparsely settled region of swamps and peat bogs. Until the 12th century, only scattered towns clung to the soggy coast. These settlements entrenched themselves — literally. Settlers began to drain swamps, dam the rivers, bolster the coastline with dikes and ditches. They wrested the land from the sea, living with the threat that it could once again be flooded. Local and regional rulers granted these towns considerable independence and autonomy.

Writers have pondered the question of Amsterdam's meteoric rise to power. Poets and scholars speculated that this perpetual struggle with the sea forged a people with energy, persistence, ingenuity and daring. Furthermore, the region was set apart from the old patterns of European thought and had no history of encrusted traditions. The region had some definite advantages as well. Several important rivers from the interior of northern Europe reached the sea here. There was maritime access to Scandinavia as well as to the riches of Russia and Germany, and, through wars with Denmark, it solidified control of northern sea lanes. Agricultural land was rich and fish were plentiful. Peat provided cheap fuel, and wind provided power. One of its first spurts of economic growth came in the 14th century when Amsterdam was designated a toll way for foreign beer. Beer was a popular drink and an alternative to contaminated water. The beer cargoes passed through Amsterdam, which became a transit point for Baltic grain. Because it handled the flow of foodstuffs from all over Europe, Amsterdam could capitalize on regional shortages and surpluses.

The city received a religious boost when, after 1345, news of the 'Miracle of the Host' spread. A dying man, it seems, was given the sacrament of Holy Communion, but he was unable to swallow it. The undigested sacrament was thrown into a fire, and was later discovered untouched by the flames. A chapel was built on the spot in the Kalverstraat. Pilgrims began flocking to the holy place and with them came added revenue.

The Amstel River, the only natural river in the area, was dammed and diverted in the late 13th century, creating an entry for ships where the river mouth had been. The city revolved around the dam: the name Amsterdam is derived from 'dam on the Amstel'. The customs house and a new church were built on the dam. The city soon developed along both banks of the Amstel. Some streets and canals followed the route of agricultural ditches and paths. As houses increased in size, foundations were made by sinking clusters of wooden piles deep down into the layers of sand. A regulation in the mid-15th century ordered replacement of easily inflammable board and thatch with stone facing, slate and tile.

With the voyages of discovery, the 16th century heralded the opening of new horizons. Expeditions probed the seas for global trade routes, discovering new lands and strange cultures. With extended trade, the mercantile system developed, with trading nations vying for mastery. Although the Portuguese were the masters of the distant trade routes, Amsterdam, with its well-developed urban center, available labor and excellent port, became the hub in a network of channels through which flowed wood, furs, fish, spices and cloth. By the first half of the 16th century, Amsterdam had become a major cloth center, with cloth being produced in the households of the poor who were already streaming to the city from the countryside. Amsterdam became the center in a series of lowland Dutch towns and cities connected through an intricate network of inland waterways along which plied barges loaded with goods.

The 16th century also brought waves of religious dissent which shook the foundations of the Catholic Church. Amsterdam, a city permeated with Catholicism, was rocked with reform and heretical movements. The Calvinists achieved the strongest foothold, and their increasing strength was aimed against the Catholic Church as well as the local oligarchical rule. King Philip II of Spain, whose rule extended to the Netherlands, including what is now Belgium, took repressive measures against the Protestants in the north. He even introduced the Inquisition which had so terrorized Spain. The Netherlands provinces united in resistance, and an expedition sent to quell the rebellion brutally sacked Antwerp in 1576. This act resulted in increased and united resistance. The northern provinces proclaimed independence in 1579, forming the Republic of the United Provinces under William of Orange as hereditary stadholder. Of the seven provinces united in the republic, Holland was the wealthiest, and within Holland, Amsterdam was undoubtedly the leading city.

In what became known as the Alteration, the city's Catholic rulers were expelled in 1578. In a symbolic exile they were cast off into the harbor in a boat, but they were allowed to land and quietly return to the city. Power now lay firmly in the hands of the Calvinists. They appropriated all church holdings and stripped them of decoration and imagery which they considered defiling. Many church buildings were turned into public institutions; however, much of the populace remained Catholic. Catholic churches and prayer services were forbidden, but the 'hidden' churches of the Catholics became an open secret, and were tolerated if they were unobtrusive.

In their attack on Antwerp, the Spanish crippled the port which now fell into their control. This resulted in increased activity in the newly independent port of Amsterdam. Raw materials and merchandise poured into the city, as did immigrants from the south. These included many belonging to minority Christian sects and Jews. Immigrant merchants and craftsmen brought their skills and acumen to the expanding city. Jewish diamond workers, for example, founded the diamond industry. The growth was spectacular. At the start of the 16th century the city had a population of 12,000 but by the end of the century the number had increased to 50,000.

The Dutch were by now master sailors. Their shipbuilding yards were unrivalled. The Dutch East India Company became the driving force behind the unprecedented expansion. The expeditions of the Company ended the Portuguese monopoly on trade. The East India Company founded the colony of Batavia on Java in 1619, drove the Portuguese from Malacca in 1641, and took control of Indonesia from the English. Semi-precious metals, luxury goods, coffee, tea, carpets, and other goods poured into Amsterdam, bringing great profits.

Its western counterpart, the Dutch West India Company, faced a strong English and French presence in the western hemisphere, and had limited success in founding and holding colonies. Nevertheless, the network of Dutch shipping controlled trade. Their cargo included thousands of black slaves shipped from Africa to North America.

The city was ruled through a system of four burgomasters. Power was tightly held by a few men, with positions interconnected in a manner which made the transfer of power all but impossible.

*I*NTRODUCTION

Citizenship was conferred according to wealth, and this lay in the hands of the merchants. These burgomasters exalted their positions and saw themselves as leaders of a new society. Although reality fell short of this vision, the city was, in many fields, progressive. The half-moon grid of canals facilitated the transfer of goods right to the storerooms, and the geometric pattern of the city, which fitted so well into the surrounding countryside, was marvelled at by 17th-century visitors.

Part of Amsterdam's glorified view of its role in the world was a sense of responsibility for the unfortunate. Poverty was prevalent in the pre-industrial city. Numerous charities were set up, and there was encouragment, both official and unofficial, to contribute towards the welfare of the poor. By the 18th century, schools were set up for the children of lower class families, which were intended to defuse the problem of delinquency and street gangs. The concern for hygiene and cleanliness was evident throughout the city. By the 18th century, executions under the Dutch court system were rare, and productive labor for prisoners replaced the floggings and similar punishments found in other systems.

Amsterdam's Golden Age tarnished quickly. By the latter half of the 17th century the momentum of growth had slowed. England and France began to effectively counter Dutch trade monopolies. Nieuw Amsterdam, in North America, was taken by the English and became New York. France invaded the Netherlands under Louis XIV and came so close to capturing Amsterdam that the Dutch were forced to open the dikes on the French, and on themselves.

By the 18th century, Amsterdam had lost its lead in shipping and building. The Dutch East India Company ran into serious problems, due to overextended credit and misappropriation of funds by company controllers. The Dutch West India Company had already been greatly reduced in its trading power. As industries developed, some moved out of the city to places where cheaper labor could be found. There were internal uprisings against the 'tax farmers', but Amsterdam's lower classes still had a comparatively high standard of living, and its well-organized social institutions remained. There was still a sense of tolerance among its rich ethnic mixture.

Now a smaller and weaker power, the Netherlands needed to play the delicate game of capitalizing on the weaknesses and vacuums that appeared within the larger competition between England, France and a rising Germany. Its vulnerable land and its navy, however, was often under attack.

INTRODUCTION

The impact of the French Revolution did not take long to reach Amsterdam. The newly formed democratic movement in the Netherlands asked the new French government to help unseat the old regime in Amsterdam. However, under the French, who had been welcomed as liberators in 1795, trade and shipping almost came to a halt because of Napoleon's restrictive trade polices. He handed over the now impoverished republic to his brother Louis, making it the Kingdom of Holland. Louis sequestered the Town Hall and, ironically, turned it into the Royal Palace. Thus, under French rule, Amsterdam, and the Netherlands as a whole, were economically drained; its maritime power was broken, its trade links severed, and its resources exhausted.

In 1813, after the defeat of Napoleon, the French were expelled from the Netherlands. The Netherlands became a constitutional monarchy under William I, with Amsterdam as its capital. Amsterdam was no longer a semi-independent entity, but part of a state, subject to state control and state policy. The protectionist trade policies, which had buffered Amsterdam from its sister Dutch cities as much as from outside national competitors, were now dismantled, and although Amsterdam was still titled the capital of the Netherlands, the actual seat of government was in The Hague.

After the period of French rule, the Netherlands was gradually able to reclaim some of its colonies. Shipping improved, and Amsterdam again became a center for world trade. There was a strengthening and extension of Amsterdam's services as a banking center. In the mid-19th century the opening of the Suez Canal drastically reduced the sailing time to the eastern colonies, and Amsterdam became an important exporter of Dutch merchandise. Amsterdam's harbor, however, could not handle the newer, bigger ships as easily as Rotterdam's could. Rotterdam had access to the Rhine, and formed a convenient bridge between the rapidly industrializing regions in Great Britain and the Ruhr Valley in Germany. Thus Rotterdam became the largest port in the world, supplanting Amsterdam as an international trading center. Amsterdam became the key city in a string of urban communities that stretched along the whole coast of the Netherlands down to Rotterdam. The Centraal Station, built on a series of islands around the harbor, transformed Amsterdam from a maritime to a railroad hub.

By the second half of the 19th century, Amsterdam was developing into a modern industrial city. Immigrants from the rural areas came in search of work in the new factories, and between 1850 and 1900 the population doubled to 500,000. New districts were built to house the influx of workers and the more comfortable middle class, while the center of the city deteriorated, with families often crowded into dark, dank, tiny basements. There was also an increase in social programs, accompanied by the laying of basic municipal services and an emphasis on education for all strata of society. Paralleling the growth of the middle class and the extension of voting rights, there arose a strong labor movement.

During World War I, Holland clung to its status as a non-belligerent nation and was spared the horrible butchery which afflicted most of Europe. Dutch shipping, however, was affected, and the country suffered economic deprivation. After the war, in a move towards greater self-sufficiency, the country pursued reclamation projects in the Zuider Zee to provide more agricultural land. The Netherlands, and Amsterdam in particular, were hard hit by unemployment during the depression of the 1930s. The Dutch government managed to contain the poverty, by providing public assistance, subsidizing farming and creating public works programs. One of these programs entailed the sending of large numbers of unemployed people to Germany, where the huge arms build up was providing jobs. In an effort to maintain strict neutrality, and because of the economic strain of the 1930s, Holland in no way strenghtened its defenses, which consequently remained weak while storm clouds gathered across the German border. The Dutch hoped that their system of water channels would provide a buffer against attack.

The Germans invaded the country in May 1940 and flattened the city of Rotterdam with bombardment. Queen Wilhelmina fled to London to rule her government in exile. The army surrendered in a matter of days. The Dutch response to German conquest was mixed. While there was a strong resistance movement in which thousands lost their lives, there was collaboration as well, with numerous volunteers for the army, for the local office of the S.S., and for the Dutch police working under the Germans.

Even with the allied invasion of Normandy in 1944, it was a long, bitter struggle to liberate the northern coastal territories. The allies were stopped at the Rhine. The campaign to push a corridor to Arnheim was thwarted. Deportations of the Jews continued into the fall of 1944. The allied advance was renewed in the spring, but Amsterdam was not liberated until just before the war's end in May 1945.

The years following the war were devoted to the long process of recovery and rebuilding. There were numerous urban, industrial, agricultural and hydraulic development projects. In 1953 during winter storms, the sea flooded vast areas of the coastal lowlands, killing some 1,800 people and causing enormous damage. This disaster gave impetus to projects to dam off certain areas. The plan for reclamation of land from the Zuider Zee north of Amsterdam was also pushed through.

There was an influx of immigrants from colonies and former colonies. A rich, cosmopolitan diversity of art and culture bloomed. In the 1960s, a new spirit of radicalism, protest and wild creativity swept across the city, especially with the rise of the Provo movement. Their happenings sprouted around the city, especially in the area of the Spui. The group was anti-big-business, anti-big-government and anti-police. One of their imaginative proposals was to ban auto traffic in the central city, which would be replaced by city-supplied white bicycles. Their activity in 1965-66 brought a violent police reaction, especially when smoke bombs were hurled at the wedding procession of Princess Beatrix. The Provos gained enough support to win a city council slot in 1966, but they and other groups faded out.

Amsterdam become one of Europe's major focal points for hippies and political radicals. Thousands of youths migrated between the Vondel park, the Dam Square and the old dairy at the Melkweg, where they could enjoy music, happenings and marijuana.

Grassroots groups also proliferated. For example, when the city proposed a subway line through the old Nieuwmarkt neighborhood, the young, arty and low-income neighborhood protested that this would drain the life from the central city for the sake of big business. The conflict led to sit-ins, mass demonstrations, and violent raids by the police on tenants and supporters who refused to leave the condemned buildings.

The metro did ultimately go through, but the Nieuwmarkt area was rebuilt in the process, with square modern apartment buildings cutting a sharp contrast to the narrow, old canal houses nearby. The Nieuwmarkt conflict highlighted the question of the fate of the old inner city, as well as the city's increasing housing problems.

City Lay-Out and Architecture

The Dam Square was, and is, truly the center of the city, physically, socially, financially and historically.

*I*NTRODUCTION

The canals, from the innermost to the outermost, are the Singel, the Herengracht, the Keizersgracht, the Prinsengracht and the Singelgracht. There are newer canals beyond, but these are the oldest canals, defining what was basically the perimeter of the 17th-century city. Within the large arc formed by these canals, most of the major attractions are found. These canals are connected by small alleys and streets, as well as by smaller canals.

The arc of the canals follows an east-west path. To the west of the Dam run two major pedestrian shopping malls on very old streets, the Nieuwendijk and the Kalverstraat which meet at the Dam Square. Further out in the same direction is the Anne Frankhuis, and beyond that the Jordaan neighborhood, the one-time working-class district which is now a modern bohemian district. To the east of the Dam Square, across the Damrak, lies the very oldest section of the city. It is now partly charming and partly red-light district.

Continuing beyond the Dam Square, on streets radiating from it, lie the Leidseplein and the Rembrandtsplein. These are the two major centers of the city's nightlife. A little beyond the Leidseplein are the Vondelpark, a famous gathering spot for the hippie invasions during the 60s, and the Museumplein, where the city's best-known museums are concentrated. The area across the Amstel River just east of Rembrandtsplein was once a densely populated Jewish Quarter, which centered around the Waterlooplein (which is next to the Visserplein).

Although water can be seen everywhere, the Amstel River is actually the only natural waterway here. The Dam Square is the spot where the Amstel was dammed; it was also sluiced, re-directed and tapped, so as to be almost unrecognizable as a natural river. The Damrak was once the waterway from the harbor and sea that ran up to the Dam. The Dam served as a barrier between river and harbor mouth, with the Amstel re-routed around it. This defined the earliest sectors of the city. The Singel, today the innermost canal, was once the outermost canal, but the network was steadily expanded as the city grew and prospered.

The canals had no small role in spurring that prosperity. From the time of their construction they served several functions: defense, efficient land (or water) use, public transport and commerce. The canals opened the city to trade. Goods could be handled easily, and transferred directly from ship to warehouse. Enterprising citizens with a little extra attic space for storage could, with a fairly low investment, launch a trading business.

INTRODUCTION

Many a merchant grew wealthy through plying the canals with his goods, and, in what became typical Amsterdam fashion, physical form and function were beautifully blended. The canals were not only planned efficiently, but gracefully. They were lined with trees, and spanned by arched bridges. They enhanced the city with a village like charm that is alive today and central to the city's character.

This applies to the architecture of the old houses as well. From the canals or the streets, differences in the various gables can be clearly seen. The gable began as a practical feature, the juncture of steeply sloped wooden roofs that prevented snow from collecting and that were appropriate to the narrow houses. The houses were built narrow because of the preciousness of the reclaimed land, and the taxing system, which valued the house by width. When wood was replaced by brick, through city ordinance, to prevent fires (fires severely damaged the early city), the gables continued as an architectural feature, but developed tremendously in design. There are at least nine separate styles of gable, with such variations as the step gable, spout gable, bell gable, etc. They were not only imaginatively shaped but ornately bordered. The gables became the individual expression of a house and a house's owner. While the facades of even wealthy houses were kept relatively sober, the gables could be frilly and covered with friezes, curls, swirls, wreaths, wings, busts, angels, and even statuettes of dolphins and sea gods.

Protruding from the center of the gable — again in both the simplest and most splendid houses — were hoisting beams. Supporting a system of ropes and winches, these beams were used to hoist goods and furniture outside the house, since the stairs were often too narrow, steep and numerous to negotiate. Goods could be raised directly from barges on the canals. Even today, these beams are used. And, like the gables themselves, the hoisting beams were made to be attractive.

One of the most remarkable features of the Amsterdam canal house is one which cannot be seen — the foundation. To provide sufficient support in the soggy, swampy soil, clusters of wooden piles were driven in deep. The Royal Palace stands on a foundation of over 13,000 such piles! While some houses were built at a slight tilt forward, to ease the hoisting and lowering of goods, others slant precipitously forward, clearly the result of sinking and a foundering of the foundation.

Strolling along the canals, you'll not miss the gablestones: sculpted images in round, square or rectangular frames above the lintel of the front entrance. They are funny, pretty, elaborate, sober or imaginative, and they even served a function, namely to provide some sort of indication as to the house's owner (in lieu of address numbers). Stones depicting bakers, hatmakers, coffee importers, etc., describe the owner's occupation. They are shaped in meticulous detail, showing just the appropriate tools that a craftsman might use.

Gablestones often referred to popular allegories or legends, or to biblical scenes. Above the front entrance of an apple-dealer the scene of Adam and Eve with snake and apple is portrayed. The gablestones contained puns and riddles. A frieze of a hand on a rooster hung above the door of a man named Hancock, and the stone of a man surrounded by lions probably represented a Mr. Daniels. The artists could be highly imaginative with these miniature panoramas, creating trees and people upside down, or a barrelmaker standing in one of his barrels.

Amsterdam's gablestones have been officially preserved, so that when a building is demolished, efforts are made to save the gablestone and remount it. Groups of them can be found on brick walls, such as the north end of Oudezijds Voorburgwal, and on Sint Luciensteeg near the Amsterdam Historical Museum. More than simply historical artifacts, these stones help paint a picture of city life during Amsterdam's rise to power. A collection of stones depicting fruits and vegetables indicate the one-time presence of a produce market. Portrayals of craftsmen busy at their crafts illustrate their methods and implements; the numerous biblical scenes hint at the pervasive sense of religion.

Even after the appearance of house numbers, the tradition of gablestones has been carried on. More recent ones are often more bizarre and whimsical than their forebearers, having only an aesthetic purpose. Some exceptional ones can be found in and around the Jordaan neighborhood, where many artists and students live.

Land and Water

The city of Amsterdam, like most of the surrounding countryside, has been literally wrested from the water. The feats of Dutch hydraulic engineering and manipulation are ingenious. Even in recent decades, farm land has been claimed from the sea. The methods and principles are often quite similar to those first applied by fishermen in the 12th century, but with the aid of advanced technology. Over half of Holland's dry land mass, in fact has been reclaimed from marsh, low lakes, estuaries or

*I*NTRODUCTION

the sea itself. On a drive or bicycle ride through the lush green Dutch farmland you will be amazed at the intricate maze of dikes and inland water channels, some supporting vessels that are quite large.

Where it began, how it began, how these immense projects were executed in the tumultuous North Sea itself, is quite mind-boggling.

The low-lying plots of farmland are known as polders. A series of dikes are first dug around these water-covered areas and beyond the dikes, and the dikes are backed by drainage canals. Water is then pumped from the squared-off region into the canals on the other side of the dikes, creating a lush, organically rich plot of dry (or soggy) land that is actually sunk below the level of the surrounding drainage canals. These canals are wide and deep enough to support fair-sized ships, and it is a strange feeling to drive along a road at the edge of a polder, by a dike, and glance up to see sails, masts and hulls above the level of the road. Water constantly seeps back into these polders and must be constantly pumped out. The quaint windmills that dot the countryside (the 950 that remain are all national monuments) were actually ingenious pumping stations. Lined up along the canals, and gracing the skyline of every town and village, they kept the country dry. The combination of hydraulic engineering and wind engineering literally created a landscape and a country.

The pumping is now done electrically, in a never-ending struggle to keep the acreage dry and exposed. If, for some reason, the pumping system broke down, the polders would be immersed within weeks. The Netherlands then, must work constantly, just to keep itself above the water level.

The Zuider Zee, the long tidal arm of the North Sea that stretched around Holland's western peninsula to Amsterdam itself, was closed off in the 1930s by an amazing feat of hydraulic engineering, the Afsluitdijk. This long dike built across the Zuider Zee transformed the eastern part into a huge freshwater lake called the IJsselmeer, and created immense new polders to the nation's land mass. The dike is bolstered with huge rocks and topped by a four-lane highway, with the waves of the North Sea slamming smack up against it. But even these imaginative and superbly built projects do not protect the country absolutely against the violence of the sea. As late as 1953, massive gales and flooding combined to wash over land and villages. After that disaster, which killed 1800 people, the Dutch mobilized their determination and engineering know-how to weave into the nation's shoreline of estuaries a series of barriers that would block the sea. The capstone of these efforts is the huge surge barrier recently completed across the long Oosterschelde estuary. Once again, the challenge was colossal and Dutch engineers met it, with radical new designs in everything from sea-floor foundations to dam structure. It's a long way from the story of the boy who plugged the dike with his fingers (a legend more popular abroad than in Holland) or wooden windmills, but the challenge is the same: how to keep the sea out and a land alive.

Dutch Art

Dutch art flourished in the 17th century, and paintings of high quality were produced in great quantities. There were particular circumstances which fostered a Dutch style of art which was quite different from the prevailing Baroque art in Europe.

The traditional patrons of Baroque art were the church and royalty, but in the 17th century, Calvinism was firmly established in Holland, and therefore imagery in church buildings was not acceptable. Furthermore there was no monarchy or traditional aristrocracy, so the traditional patrons of Baroque art were not to be found in Holland. However, there was a wealthy bourgeois class, and for the first time artists began to work independently on a free market. The country was prosperous, with overseas colonies and flourishing worldwide trade. The demand for paintings suddenly grew, and enormous numbers of good paintings were produced.

Most of these paintings were small enough to hang in a living room. There were almost no religious or mythological compositions. Not many Biblical scenes were painted, and these were mostly set in terms of everyday life. The Dutch painters depicted narratives, allegorical scenes, and scenes of daily life and the local environment. These paintings concentrated on upper-middle-class settings, interiors and gardens, still lifes, taverns and people absorbed in leisure activities.

Three Dutch masters in the 17th century rose above the generally high level to achieve universal recognition: Rembrandt, Hals and Vermeer.

Rembrandt Harmenszoon van Rijn (1606-69) was the most creative and influential Dutch artist of the 17th century, and one of the greatest artists of all time. His paintings, etchings and drawings reveal unsurpassed control of technique, light, shadow and color, and a deep knowledge of body movements, gestures and expressions, which convey the very essence of the subject matter.

Rembrandt's work and identity are as closely tied to Amsterdam as Dickens is to London. Rembrandt made moving sketches of his home life, and also marvelous studies of life going on about him in Amsterdam. The characters in the streets, their gestures and costumes, were used many times in his paintings. Here he spent most of his life and made and lost his fortune. He absorbed the atmosphere of the city in all its rich variety and burgeoning vitality, and painted the city's wealthy, the beggars, Calvinists, Mennonites and Jews.

The merchants and civic leaders who made Amsterdam the richest city in the world had a strong urge to immortalize their city, their families and themselves in paintings and etchings. Artists were respected professionals who deserved recompense for good work, and a popular artist could grow very wealthy from his work. Amsterdam became an international marketplace for art as it did for everything else. In this setting, the drama of one of the greatest artists of all time unfolded.

Rembrandt was born in 1606 to a middle-class family in Leiden, the son of a miller. He showed an early talent for drawing, and was trained as a painter in Amsterdam. He spent a few years in Leiden, and then returned to Amsterdam. From his first days there, he gained a good reputation as a portrait painter. Commissions poured in, including from the House of Orange. Rembrandt married Saskia van Uylenburgh, the daughter of a wealthy family, bought an elegant house in a respectable district, and his career seemed made.

His life, however, was filled with tragedy. Within seven years, from 1636 to 1642, he lost three infants, his mother and his wife Saskia. Later he lost his beloved mistress and his only son to reach maturity. In addition to suffering these tragedies in his personal life, Rembrandt also got into serious financial trouble, and was even forced to sell his house, although he continued to receive important commissions. In spite of these difficulties, Rembrandt's creative powers grew and developed.

Every medium and technique that Rembrandt used, he studied, absorbed and shaped into something exclusively his own, capturing the emotions and the souls of human beings. He portrayed dignity in a beggar, suffering in a Jew, affluent society figures, and important personalities. His group portraits reached a new level, with depth, drama and individual expressions in each character.

*I*NTRODUCTION

His paintings have great psychological intensity, and dramatic use of light and shade. Rembrandt seems to have been influenced by Caravaggio's dramatic contrasts of light and dark, and by Rubens' spiral composition and speed of execution.

Steeped in the Bible since youth, Rembrandt used his wide knowledge and understanding in many moving paintings of religious subjects. One of his most dramatic paintings of a religious subject is *Angel Leaving Tobit and Tobias* (The Louvre, Paris). In the apocryphal story, blind Tobit has his sight restored by the Archangel Raphael. Tobit prostrates himself in gratitude, while his son looks up in wonder at the departing angel. The angel flies off into a flash of light. His later religious pictures became deeper and more tranquil. In the *Supper at Emmaus* (The Louvre, Paris), Christ reveals himself to two of his disciples. The picture is gently illumined by rays from Christ's head, and only the slightest movements of the two disciples reveal their recognition of Christ.

Rembrandt created some unsurpassed etchings, dealing with landscape, daily life and religious subjects. Often the etchings went through several stages before he was satisfied with them. One of the most famous is *The Three Crosses* (The Metropolitan Museum of Art, New York).

The master who had captured the spirit in so many faces, similarly captured the many faces inherent within his own feautures. The Baroque was a period which excelled in self-portraits, and Rembrandt painted many self-portraits, with increasing depth, as his difficult and often tragic life forced him to change his self-assessment. He painted himself in wide brimmed hats with feathers, in jewels and gold braid. We see Rembrandt as social dabbler and social misfit, as tramp, clown, philosopher king, saint, and as the patient, dedicated craftsman. Even his later self-portraits, while revealing double chins and hanging cheeks, retain their sense of strength, determination and acceptance.

Frans Hals (1581/85-1666) was one of the greatest 17th-century Dutch artists, and a most brilliant portaitist. His interest was in the human face and figure. He had an unmatched gift for catching the individual in a moment of action, capturing a fleeting expression or mood. His portraits are thus a complete contrast from the calm and deliberately composed portraits of the great Renaissance painters.

His genius is apparent in his group portrait *Banquet of the Officers of the Saint George Guard Company* (Frans Hals

*I*NTRODUCTION

Museum, Haarlem). Rather than assembling the 12 figures in a formal group, Hals has painted them informally gathered around a table, jovial and relaxed.

The Laughing Cavalier (Wallace Collection, London) shows a gallant and confident young man, with a dashing costume and hat. Hals has captured all the details of his costume, hat, hair and moustache with brilliant brushwork, but most of all it is the lively and amorous expression of the cavalier which makes this painting so outstanding.

In old age Hals' genial warmth was replaced by a more sombre outlook, as can be seen in another group portrait, *Regentesses of the Old Men's Almhouse* (Frans Hals Museum, Haarlem). This composition is calm, solemn and austere, but Hals has still captured the individuality of each character in the group portrait.

Jan Vermeer (1632-75) was another master among Dutch painters. His output was small, only some 35 paintings, nearly all of which are interiors. His works do not have a strong emotional or dramatic content, but he transformed simple actions into timeless symbols. His paintings achieve a noble calmness through perfectly adjusted spatial relationships, tone and color.

His interiors are almost always lit from a small side window, and it has been suggested that he used a camera obscura in preliminary studies of light and perspective for his compositions.

In his painting *Kitchen Maid* (Rijksmuseum, Amsterdam) the colors of the maid's clothes are harmoniously reflected in the other colors of the room. Vermeer has created a monumental composition out of this quiet and tranquil moment.

Vermeer made a study of optics, and in his few outdoor landscapes the glowing intensity of his colors reached a new level. In his *View of Delft* (Mauritshuis, The Hague), he has brilliantly captured the weight of the clouds, the diffused light, the moist air and the subtle tonal differences. The small figures are part of a calm and beautiful scene.

Vincent Van Gogh (1853-90) was a Post-Impressionist painter who used art primarily as a means of emotional expression. Before turning to painting, Van Gogh worked as a language teacher, was a student of practical evangelism and a missionary to coal-miners in a poverty stricken village. In these brief careers, and also in many of his personal relationships, he showed a deep love of humanity and of life, but he experienced at the same time a sense of failure and betrayal. This intensely personal feeling is revealed in his work, and seems to attain in some of his

*I*NTRODUCTION

works an inspired or even religious intensity. Van Gogh suffered from bouts of mental illness and died an untimely death, but he achieved a stature comparable with the great Dutch artists of the 17th century.

His earliest works are figure drawings of miners and peasants in northern Holland. He only commenced formal art studies at the age of 28. In 1886 he came to Paris, and, under the influence of the Impressionists and Japanese prints, he began to use brighter color and a new sense of pattern. Suffering from depression, he moved to Arles in Provence, where, between 1886-88 he produced a series of masterpieces flooded by intense sunlight, and enraptured by the beauty of the landscape. *A View of La Crau* (Van Gogh Museum, Amsterdam) is a typical example. With its thick pigment, blazing color and strong brushstrokes, it typifies Van Gogh's Post-Impressionist style. This particular picture is extremely tranquil and peaceful.

This series of pictures was followed by some highly disturbing works. The famous *Night Cafe* (Yale University Art Gallery, New Haven, Connecticut) is one example, where Van Gogh deliberately distorted perspective and used harshly contrasting colors to convey the idea 'that the cafe is a place where one can ruin oneself, run mad or commit a crime. So I have tried to express, as it were, the powers of darkness in a low drink shop...' (from one of Van Gogh's letters).

After an attack of mental instability, Van Gogh spent some time at an asylum in Saint-Remy, where he continued to paint. His self-portraits are deeply searching and show his hard-won triumph over profound sorrow. *Starry Night* (Museum of Modern Art, New York) was painted at this time, and is not so much a visual record of what he saw — with its swirling masses of color and exploding light — as it is a visionary and ecstatic expression.

Van Gogh died at the age of 37, two days after shooting himself in the abdomen. His brother Theo, who supported him financially and encouraged his painting, died six months later, and was buried beside Van Gogh at Auvers-sur-Oise.

INTRODUCTION

Part Two — Setting Out

How to get there

By air: There are connections between Amsterdam's main airport, Schiphol, and all major European airports. There are also regular flights several times weekly from North America, Australia, and South Africa. KLM, the Dutch national airline, flies to and from 76 countries.

By train: Overseas visitors who intend to do a lot of traveling by rail around continental Europe may be interested in purchasing a Eurailpass. This unlimited-mileage ticket is valid for first-class travel practically anywhere in western Europe, except Great Britain. Anyone under 26 can get the second-class Eurail Youthpass. These tickets must be bought outside Europe. The Interrail Pass is available to anyone under 16 and to women over 60 and men over 65 and is on sale in Europe. It entitles its bearer to one month's transport throughout 19 European countries (at half-fare in the country of issue and free in the other countries).

By sea: Amsterdam can be reached by boat, but more usually tourists arrive by the many ferry services which are offered from various points in Europe, particularly England. There is also a car ferry from England.

Documents and customs regulations

To enter Holland from most countries, only a valid passport is needed. If coming from certain distant countries, a smallpox vaccination may be necessary, and this should be checked with a local travel agent, a KLM officer or the Dutch embassy before departure for Holland. Young travelers who appear to be roughing it are sometimes stopped at passport control and given a mild interrogation. They are usually asked if they know anyone in the country, how long they intend staying and if they have any money. For such emergencies, a credit card can do wonders, even if you have no intention of using it.

A word of warning: Holland's liberal laws concerning marijuana and hashish are well-known (see 'Drugs'), but import of these drugs is controlled, so do not bring any of your own as you may find the response less than liberal.

INTRODUCTION

There are no restrictions on the import or export of currency from Holland, but check for possible restrictions in your own country. Certain quantities of duty-free cigarettes, cigars, tobacco, liquors and wine are allowed into the Netherlands. These quantities differ for EEC and non-EEC countries, with visitors from non-EEC countries being allowed more. These figures should be checked at your airport before departure for Holland.

Insurance

Medical insurance when traveling abroad is a necessity, whether made through a health plan or through an insurance or travel agent. The Netherlands has reciprocal emergency care agreements with a number of European countries, such as England. British citizens, to activate this agreement, must obtain certificate E111. Check with your own health plan to see what the extent of coverage is. Americans must usually buy extra medical insurance for abroad. Make sure to keep all medical bills — and, if involved in an accident, keep a copy of the police report as well.

Insurance against theft is also a good idea. Remember that there are many skillful pick-pockets in Amsterdam.

When to come; national holidays

The weather in Amsterdam is consistent only in its inconsistency. Summer days can be hot and dry, or hot and muggy after the rain. Sometimes they are bright, sometimes cool and windy, and at other times there can be chilly showers. It may not rain at all, but one should always be prepared for it.

Winters are also unpredictable with blizzards, light snow, or sunshine. Winds can whip in off the North Sea, and the canals freeze over. People skate on the canals and cars do drive on them, though this not recommended. There is something very special and magical about a visit to Amsterdam in the winter. In the winter, rates drop in many hotels, but some attractions may reduce their hours or close completely.

The tourist season begins in late spring with the tulip season and the various attendant festivals. Although the endless acres of tulip fields are mainly south of Haarlem, Amsterdam is obviously a major stop and joins in the spirit of the flowery celebrations.

By the beginning of summer, the visitors stream into Amsterdam, but the density of the crowds fluctuates.

During the autumn, there is an influx of business visitors for

Amsterdam's spate of conventions and conferences, but they do not really influence the overall tourist market.

Below is a list of national holidays:

New Year	1 January
Good Friday	Friday preceeding Easter (most shops are open)
Easter	March/April (varies)
Queen's Birthday	30 April (most shops are open in the morning)
Ascension Day	40th day after Easter
Whitsun	The week beginning with Whit Sunday, the 7th Sunday after Easter
Liberation Day	5 May, a public holiday every five years, next in 1990
Remembrance Day	4 May, in memory of the victims of World War II, not a public holiday
Christmas	25 December

What to wear

Because of the unpredictable weather, it can be a little tricky deciding what to bring. In any season, one should always be prepared with an umbrella and raincoat. Likewise, it is always wise to bring at least one heavy sweater. In winter, when temperatures drop, a real winter wardrobe is needed.

In a city like Amsterdam, a comfortable pair of walking shoes is essential. Take at least one pair of heavier and warmer socks, for that unexpected chill or rain.

It is preferable, of course, to bring a pair of shoes that provide protection against the rain, but that is not always practical, especially in summer. If you are caught in an endless downpour do as the locals do and buy a pair of wooden clogs with leather or some other kind of protective top, to be worn with a pair of thick socks.

As for style, a little bit of everything is found in Amsterdam, from faded jeans and open workshirts, to leather and glitter, to elegant sports jackets and suits. Some of the fancier hotels will require at least a sports jacket and tie, and perhaps a dress for a women, so take at least one better outfit for that night on the town.

INTRODUCTION

How much will it cost?

Budget, naturally, depends on many personal factors, but there are some general guidelines. Amsterdam offers a wide range of prices in all tourist services.

From the Airport: A taxi to the city center costs between 40-60 fl; by bus you will pay 10 fl, and by train, 4.40 fl.

Hotels: A luxury hotel starts at 300 fl. First-class hotels, some of which lean toward the luxury end in facilities, cost from 200-350 fl. A comfortable, upper-medium range room could cost from 125-200 fl. A simpler, but pleasant room with private bath goes from about 90-150 fl. More spartan budget singles, without baths, start at 40 fl. Student-type accommodation starts at 20 fl, though there are a few places which offer a mattress on a floor and cost even less.

Eating Out: Restaurants show the same variation. One might easily spend 30 fl on lunch and 45-60 fl on dinner, in a restaurant or bistro which is nice but not especially elegant. 20-25 fl is the average price for a full-course meal. However, the budget-conscious traveler can eat well for about 12 fl in small, simple restaurants, or fill up on pizza, which starts at 10 fl and will satisfy two. Sandwiches start at 4 fl.

Local Transportation: This will likely be a low expense. A public-transport ticket costs 1.70 fl, an all day ticket about 10 fl. For two days, it's about 15 fl. Because the city is so compact, you may not need to use public transportation much.

Bicycle Rental: Costs about 8 fl per day, with deposits ranging from 50-200 fl.

Canal boats, pedal boats: The standard canal boat ride costs about 9 fl. Fancier variations, with candlelight, snacks, meals, etc., may cost from 15-35 fl per person. The pedal boats are charged by the boat. A 2-person boat costs 16.50 fl per hour, a 4-person boat costs about 25 fl. There is a 50-75 fl deposit.

Out of the City Excursions: 25-50 fl.

Admission Fees: Most, but not all, of the major museums are covered by the Museumcard, which costs 21 fl and much less for under 25. Other sights, such as the Royal Palace, charge very modest fees, 1-3 fl. A few other attractions, such as Madame Tussaud's, charge from 5-10 fl.

*I*NTRODUCTION

Part Three — Easing the shock: Where have we landed?

Transportation

Travel Information

Amsterdam has a large selection of cheap rates by air, train and bus. There are a number of travel offices which offer special low rates. These are conveniently situated near one another along the Rokin and on the Damstraat by the Dam Square. It is very difficult to obtain the details by phone, so it is preferable to go to the office. During the summer season, there are usually long waiting lines.

Budget Air: Rokin 34, Tel. 27 12 51.

Budget Bus: Rokin 10, Tel. 27 51 51.

Pendel Express: Rokin 38, Tel. 26 44 34.

Transalpino Travel: Rokin 44, Tel. 24 74 54.

NBBS: (Student travel office), Dam 17, Tel. 23 76 86 or Tel. 23 76 87, no answer Tel. 071-22 14 14, Leidsestraat 53, Tel. 38 17 36.

Airport

Amsterdam is a hub for air traffic from around the world, and its **Schiphol Airport** is a modern, pleasant airport under one roof, located about eight miles south of the city. It provides a free nursery for children, a junior jet lounge for unaccompanied children, and large duty-free shopping facilities. There are several modern hotels around the perimeter, an aviation museum, and a meditation room.

The airport information center, located towards the middle of the lower level of the terminal, can supply basic information, especially on hotels. Money changing services are found at the baggage claim, and in the train station adjoining the airport. Free baggage carts are also located at the baggage claim.

*I*NTRODUCTION

There are several modern business-class hotels (*Hilton, Golden Tulip*) near the airport, with reservation service at the airport and reachable by free shuttle. A self-service hotel reservation center can be found just to the left of the information center. It provides direct free phone service to a number of middle to upper range hotels. It is advisable to use this service as the tourist information center is usually extremely busy with long waiting lines. There are no low-budget hotels included at the self-service reservation center.

Adjoining the airport is a train station. Train tickets are bought on the upper level of the station. Next to the ticket office is a railroad information counter. There are direct lines to The Hague and Rotterdam from this station. Trains run to the RAI station in the south of Amsterdam and to the Beethovenstraat (Amsterdam-south), as well as to the Centraal Station.

KLM also runs a bus service, costing about 2 fl, from the airport to Amsterdam's Centraal Station and Utrecht which leaves about every 20 minutes. Taxis from the airport to the city are also available as are car rentals on the main floor.

The **Aviodome**, Amsterdam's aeronautic museum, may keep you entertained while waiting for your flight. About 25 planes, including real and simulated spacecraft, survey the development of aviation and especially the role of the Netherlands. The museum is not highly recommended. (Open daily April-Oct. 10am-5pm, closed Mon. from Nov.-March. Admission 4.50 fl. Museumcard not valid. Tel. 17 36 40.)

Railway Station

The **Centraal Station** is Amsterdam's railway station. More than 1000 trains from the Netherlands and the rest of Europe arrive and depart daily. The station has the usual facilities including an information counter.

In-Town Transportation

Amsterdam has an extensive, efficient public transportation system which includes the **tram** lines, city and regional **bus** lines, and two underground **metro** lines. The transit authority is known as the GVB. The main information office is located near the VVV tourist information office at the Stationsplein.

A tourist is most likely to use the tram lines. Most of the 13 tram lines emanate from the Centraal Station, and a few run across the city. The buses run further afield, and intersect with many of the lines. The metro system mainly serves residential neighborhoods beyond the city center. The Nieuwmarkt and Waterlooplein areas are the only tourist attractions located along the metro line.

The system can be a little confusing due to the many different kinds of vehicles, and the two separate ways to purchase tickets. A map and general brochure explaining the system are available from the tourist information centers. Many of the tram and bus shelters display a map of the entire transit network. A single ticket costs 1.70 fl and can be purchased from the driver when you board a tram or bus. A ticket for one hour costs 2.55 fl.

Multiple-use tickets can be purchased, good for up to several days. A ticket that is good all day costs about 10 fl. A ticket for two days costs about 15 fl. These tickets are available from the tram and bus drivers, from the automatic ticket-dispenser in Metro stations and from the GVB information and ticket-sale points. Stamp these multiple-use tickets before your first trip. A day ticket is usually not worthwhile, while the two-day or three-day tickets are successively better deals.

There is also a strip ticket (*stripkaarten*) system, which is based on the number of zones you will travel through. Amsterdam has 11 transit zones. To use the strip ticket, you must know how many zones you will be passing through to your destination. Most tourist sights are located within the large central zone, the Centrum. You must stamp one more strip than the number of zones you are crossing. From drivers, you can buy tickets of ten strips for about 10 fl. More economical tickets with 15 strips can be purchased at GVB centers or post offices.

Strip tickets include transfers to other tram, bus or metro lines. Stamped for one, two or three zones, the ticket is valid for one hour. Passengers, including foreigners, found without a valid ticket are fined 26 fl.

Regular bus and tram service starts at about 6am and ends at 12:15am. After regular lines stop running, night buses are available, which usually run every hour throughout the night, every day of the week. Strip tickets from the day can be used on the same night. Individual tickets cost 2.50 fl. The GVB information centers provide a folder on night transportation.

Taxis in Amsterdam do not cruise looking for fares, and passing cabs do not always stop when hailed. Taxis have a black and white checkered band, and a sign on the roof, which is lit when the cab is free. The fare is calculated by the meter, except for a trip out of town, such as to the airport. The fare to the airport is about 40 fl. Tips are already included in the fare, but it is customary to round the fare up to the nearest guilder. You can order a taxi by calling the nearest taxi stand, or one central number, Tel. 77 77 77.

The Water Taxi shuttles visitors along the canals between hotels, museums, shopping centers, etc., day or night. Tel. 75 09 09.

Information/tickets

Stationsplein: Mon.-Fri. 7am-10:30pm, Sat. and Sun. 8am-10:30pm.

Leidseplein: *The Bulldog Cafe*; 8am-9:30pm, Sat. and Sun. 10:15am-5pm.

GVB Central Office: Scheepvaarthuis 108 Prins Hendrikkade. Mon.-Fri. 8:30am-4:30pm. Tel. 27 27 27.

Car Rental

The major car rental companies have offices in the center of Amsterdam and at the airport. It is generally easy to rent a car upon arrival. There is a wide range of vehicles offered for rental, from compacts to vans, and prices vary, so make a few calls first if possible. There are many small local agencies as well as the large chains. Most companies will only rent cars to drivers over 21 years. An international driver's license is necessary.

The rental of a basic compact, without mileage, starts at 50-60 fl per day, plus extra per kilometer. There are various package rates for the week and the month, with and without unlimited mileage. Insurance is extra.

Avis: 380 Nassaukade. Tel. 83 60 61.

Budget: 121 Overtoom. Tel. 12 60 66.

Disks Autoverhuur: 278-280 Van Ostadestraat. Tel. 62 33 66.

Europcar: 51-53 Overtoom. Tel. 18 45 95 or 83 21 23.

Hertz: 333 Overtoom. Tel. 12 24 41. For cars with driver, Tel. 83 16 31.

Inter Rent: 294 Amstelveenseweg. Tel. 73 04 77.

Kaspers en Lotte: 232-234 Van Ostadestraat. Tel. 71 70 66 or Tel. 71 07 33.

Kuperus B.V.: 175 Middenweg. Tel. 93 87 90.

*I*NTRODUCTION

Bicycles

Amsterdam is the bicycle capital of the world, and regardless of the weather you will see Amsterdammers from every walk of life weaving their bikes through the traffic. The amount of bicycle theft in the city is proportionately high. Some people say that as many as a hundred bicycles are stolen in Amsterdam on any given day.

Amsterdammers will joke that if your bike is stolen in the morning you can buy it back that afternoon. Riding a bike will make a visitor feel very much at home in Amsterdam. The daily rental rates are very cheap, between 6-10fl a day. But, due to the rampant theft, deposits are high, ranging from 50 to 200 fl.

Bicycle rental

Fiets-o-fiets: 880-900 Amstelveenseweg (main entrance Amsterdamse Bos). Tel. 44 54 13 or 13 16 26. 9 fl per day, deposit 200 fl.

Heja: 39 Bestevaerstraat. Tel. 12 92 11. 7 fl per day, deposit 50 fl, also mopeds 22.50 fl per day, deposit 100 fl.

Koenders: 105 Utrechtsedwarsstraat. Tel. 24 83 91. 7 fl per day, deposit 100 fl.

Rent-a-bike: 11 Pieter Jacobszdwarsstraat (near the Damstraat). Tel. 25 50 29. 7.50 fl per day, deposit 100 fl.

Rent-a-bike: 6 Stationsplein (Centraal Station). 7 fl per day, deposit 200 fl.

Zijwind: 168 Ferdinand Bolstraat. Tel. 13 15 13. 7.50 fl per day, deposit 200 fl.

Intercity Transportation

Train: The Netherlands is an excellent country to tour by rail. It is small, flat, the sights are near one another, beautiful countryside can be seen right outside the cities, and it has a dense and efficient rail network. The national rail network is known as NS, the initials for its Dutch name. The NS runs a regular schedule of trains from major stations. Amsterdam is a major rail center for both the country and the nations of northern Europe.

The information counter at the Centraal Station can answer any questions; however, there are sometimes long lines. Amsterdam's Centraal Station and other major depots will all be able to provide schedules and rate booklets, as well as pamphlets explaining what the various options of train travel are. Tickets can be bought on a one-way basis, but round-trip tickets are cheaper.

Various 'Ranger' tickets entitle the holder to unlimited travel on 3, 5 or 7 consecutive days. For a very nominal add-on price, the ticket also includes unlimited travel on public transportation (subway, trams, city and provincial buses) throughout the country. For the traveler wanting a fast but full tour of the country this is a great deal. For 120 fl, for example, one has unlimited travel on the train and public transportation systems throughout the country for one week.

Rail cars are divided into first and second class, and ticket prices vary accordingly.

NS also runs a series of day excursions which include transportation to and from a main attraction somewhere, plus entry to the attraction. Information about these excursions can be found in the pamphlet *Touring Holland By Rail*, available at any major train station. NS also runs a schedule of night trains. For information, Tel. 20 22 66, Mon.-Fri. 8am-10pm, Sat. and Sun. 9am-6pm.

Bus: Bus travel to and from Amsterdam has expanded tremendously in the last few years, especially for a younger clientele. The trip may take longer than by train, but it is usually less expensive, and a camaraderie can develop between the passengers. The buses are sleek and comfortable.

Accommodation

There is accommodation in Amsterdam for every budget. In addition to spacious, modern and stylish hotels in the first-class chains, there are the old classics, while at a lower scale there are several small family-run hotels. Many hotels are converted canal houses, with the typical steep stairs. Because of the unique character of these buildings, it is more interesting to stay in an older place than in a modern hotel, no matter how famous the name. The quaint hotels are found everywhere, along canals in every neighborhood, and many are clustered around the major tourist sights — the Leidseplein, the Rembrandtsplein, the Museumplein, the Dam Square, etc. Hotels a little further from the center tend to be a little less expensive, but this is not always the case.

Amsterdam gets very crowded in the summer and the hotels do a brisk business. There is rapid turnover, however, and it is generally possible to find a hotel room suited to any budget. Reservations are recommended in summer, at Christmas, and in the tulip season. Prices are also higher at these times, and a simple single room in a budget-class hotel, with a shared bath, could cost about 50 fl. Student hotels and hostels are, of course, cheaper. At the higher end of the scale, the prices are commensurate with similar lodgings in other cities. Rooms at a first-class hotel approach 200 fl per night for a single room.

In most hotels except the deluxe class, breakfast is included. This usually includes several kinds of meats, breads, crackers, cheeses, eggs, and sometimes cereal, fruit or fruit juice and vegetables, as well as hot beverages.

In the winter, rates in some hotels go down with the temperature, but not as sharply. If no discount is mentioned, check whether the rate quoted is the winter or summer rate. Some of the top hotels offer winter discounts approaching 40% and some hotels have special winter packages to attract guests. The National Reservation Center handles a winter package called *Amsterdam, the Amsterdam Way*. There is a set price according to the levels of the hotels, from deluxe to budget, which includes, for example, free canal cruises, free museum entry, and drinks, as well as a reduced price for additional days. Information also is available from the VVV.

In the smaller and individually-owned hotels, bathrooms and showers are not always private. Even some very comfortable hotels, at the lower end of the price range, may have shared bathroom and/or shower, so be sure to check this first.

Hotel rooms can be booked in advance through a travel agent. KLM offices will often manage bookings for hotels participating in the *Golden Tulip* reservation service.

Bookings and hotel information can also be obtained by mail through the *National Reservation Center*, which handles a wide range of hotels. P.O.Box 404, 2260 AK, Leidschendam, Holland. Tel. 070-20 25 00. Telex 33755.

As mentioned previously in the section on Schiphol Airport, there is a free self-service phone reservation office in the airport, also operated by the *National Reservation Center*. If you have not booked a room, then this service is definitely worth taking advantage of upon landing, especially during the summer or other peak traveling periods. Although the VVV runs a booking service at its main tourist information office on the Stationsplein, it is likely to be crowded. The hotels listed at the self-service counter cover a range of styles and budgets and, except for those seeking student hotels or hostels, there is something for everyone within this limited list.

At the VVV booking service at the Stationsplein, clerks will make several suggestions, show the location on a map, make the reservation by phone while you wait, and then supply directions. There is a 3 fl booking fee. The VVV offers this booking service throughout the country. In many VVV offices it is possible to make reservations for lodgings in another city, but no reservations will be made by phone.

It is possible to book boats, apartments and cabins through the National Reservation Center. It also handles bookings for bungalows, summer houses and rooms in boarding houses, but this must be done through the agency's local office. No national list of boarding houses and bed-and-breakfast type accommodation exists.

Airport Hotels

Euromotel Schiphol: 20 Oude Haagseweg, 1066 BW. Tel. 17 90 05. Singles from 125 fl, doubles from 155 fl.

Golden Tulip Schiphol: 495 Kruisweg, Hoofdorp 2132 NA. Tel. 02503-15851. Singles from 285 fl, doubles from 315 fl.

Hilton International Schiphol: Herbergierstraat, Schiphol Centrum 1118 ZK. Tel. 51 15 911. Singles from 290 fl, doubles from 350 fl.

Deluxe

American Hotel: 97 Leidsekade, 1017 PN. Tel. 24 53 22. Built with a distinctively Art-Deco American flair, it is a famous Amsterdam landmark, one step away from the Leidseplein. Its cafe is a famous gathering spot for the city's theater crowd and literati. Occasionally architecture classes pass through. Singles from 260 fl and doubles from 350 fl.

Amstel Hotel: 1 Prof. Tulpplein, 1018 GX. Tel. 22 60 60. This imposing palace-like structure on the bank of the Amstel is undoubtedly Amsterdam's most luxurious hotel, and its guest list reads like a survey of European royalty. Singles from 310 fl and doubles from 415 fl. It has full luxury hotel amenities.

Doelen Crest Hotel: 24 Nieuwe Doelenstraat, 1012 CP. Tel. 22 07 22. The oldest hotel in Amsterdam, dating back to the 17th century, it is also one of Amsterdam's finest. It is situated in a large, majestic, old building along a canal, near one of the most charming walking areas. It's perhaps the only place in the world that can claim that both Rembrandt and the Beatles passed through. The emphasis is on business clientele — singles from 253 fl and doubles from 333 fl.

Grand Hotel Krasnapolsky: 9 Dam, 1012 JS. Tel. 55 49 111. Spacious, renovated, combining old-world decor with modern comfort. The hotel faces National Monument, and has several exclusive restaurants, and a grand dining hall shaped like an aviary. Singles from 275 fl and doubles from 330 fl.

Hotel de l'Europe: 2-4 Nieuwe Doelenstraat, 1012 CP. Tel. 23 48 36. A classic 19th-century exterior with a modernised interior. It is situated on the Amstel, on a site that was a key defense point as far back as the 15th century. It has all the amenities of a luxury hotel, with a honeymoon suite in the turret. Usually appeals to business travelers or very exclusive tourists. On Christmas, it holds a dinner-dance and one night stay for only 195 fl. Normal rates are much higher with a single room from 350 fl and a double from 400 fl. Rates are lower in winter. The hotel is a member of the organization, The Leading Hotels of the World. The hotel's restaurant *Excluse Restaurant Excelsior* has won international acclaim. Located at the waterline, it offers a close-up view of passing boats.

Hotel Pulitzer: 315-331 Prinsengracht, 1016 GZ. Tel. 22 83 33. Unique among Amsterdam's hotels, the Pulitzer is composed of 19 connected old buildings, many dating from the 17th-century. The facades have been preserved intact; from the outside it is impossible to see that the interiors have been joined and revamped. The original superstructures have been meticulously preserved, and even the old beams and supports, although unseen, have been preserved. The woodwork, facades, bannisters and brick walls are all original. The hotel surrounds a pretty courtyard. None of the rooms are exactly alike, either in decor or structure. The hotel has all the usual first-class amenities, and a shuttle service between hotel and airport. Singles from 250 fl, doubles from 300 fl.

Victoria Hotel: Damrak 1-6, 1012 LG. Tel. 23 42 55. A magnificent building in the heart of the city directly opposite the Central Station. From March 1990 it will have two wings, the main building with its piano bar, marble shopping arcade and exclusive restaurant, and the new Garden Wing with fitness-centre, sauna, turkish bath jacuzzi and swimming pool. 169 rooms: singles from 230 fl, doubles from 340 fl.

First Class

Die Port Van Cleve: 178-180 Nieuwezijd Voorburgwal, 1012 SJ, Tel. 24 48 60. Although this is not one of those classic 17th-century Amsterdam buildings, the facade is phenomenal. A neoclassic masterpiece of spires, gables, dark columns, and a deep red brick background; it dates from the 19th century. It actually started as a series of restaurants and dining rooms. The ground floor, *Bodega*, is an Amsterdam landmark, with deeply polished wood paneling and a mural in Delft blue china above. The interior has been modernised, though many of the rooms have that raw-beamed rustic Dutch look. Singles start at 160 fl and doubles at 230 fl with private bath and breakfast. Rates drop in winter, just by a small amount for singles, but considerably for doubles, which start at 175 fl. A two-night package includes museum tickets, drinks, cruise, etc.

Moderate

Amsterdam Wiechman: 328-330 Prinsengracht, 1016 HX. Tel. 26 33 21. Beautiful, well-preserved setting in canal house in one of the most charming areas of town, with lovely old furnishings. Private baths available. Singles from 70 fl and doubles from 95 fl.

Canal House: 148 Keizersgracht, 1015 DX. Tel. 22 51 82. Small hotel on beautiful canal, between Jordaan and city center. It's quiet despite its central location. It has a beautiful, polished little dining room. Singles from 110 fl and doubles from 160 fl. No elevator, steep stairs.

Hotel Asterisk: 14-16 Den Texstraat, 1017 ZA. Tel. 26 23 96/ 24 17 68. A quaint, friendly and clean hotel on a quiet street, near a small green park, and across the canal from the Museumplein. Small plush lobby, pretty dining room, and prices quite reasonable compared to others of the same standard. Singles from 55 fl, doubles from 65 fl, extra with private bath.

Hotel de la Poste: 5 Reguliersgracht, 1017 LJ. Tel. 23 71 05. Lower end of moderate scale. On a very quaint canal just a short walk from the Rembrandtsplein, this hotel has only 18 rooms and has been a family run institution for three generations. Rooms are rather simple but the atmosphere is friendly and warm. Mostly doubles available, from 100 fl with bath. There are only a few singles. The rates are slightly lower in winter.

Hotel Digla: 37-39 Keizersgracht, 1015 CD. Tel. 24 96 00. On a beautiful canal, near Jordaan and Haarlemmerstraat in the old part of town. Small and old but clean. Private bath available, singles from 65 fl, doubles from 95 fl, no elevator, steep stairs.

Hotel Estherea: 303-309 Singel, 1012 WJ. Tel. 24 51 46. Quaint old canal house, central location, steep stairs, elevator, private baths. Singles from 100 fl, doubles from 140 fl. Self-service reservation from airport.

Hotel Maas: 91 Leidsekade, 1017 PN. Tel. 23 38 68. Lower end of the moderate scale. It overlooks a wide and peaceful canal, but is only two minutes from the Leidseplein. Rooms are comfortable with phone, TV and mini-bar. It has a cozy dining room and comfortable lobby, behind a pretty brown brick exterior edged with white stone. A filling buffet breakfast is served. Singles from about 60 fl and doubles from 90 fl, extra for rooms with bath.

Hotel Roemer Visscher: 10 Roemer Visscherstraat, 1054 EX. Tel. 12 55 11. A mid-sized comfortable hotel in a pleasant brick building near the Vondelpark. Pleasant management. Most rooms with bath. Self-service reservation from airport. Singles from 75 fl, doubles from 150 fl.

Hotel Westropa II: 389-390 Nassaukade, 1054 AE. Tel. 83 49 35. Sober brick exterior on a main street, across outer Singelgracht from Leidseplein. Clean, modern interior. Single with bath from 85 fl, double with bath from 125 fl. Winter discounts, as well as on Mondays and Tuesdays during the summer.

Budget

Hotel Van Onna: 102-108 Bloemgracht, 1015 TN. Tel. 26 58 01. Squeezed into an old building in the Jordaan with very steep stairs and lots of crazy angles. Bright spacious rooms at the top. Definitely budget-class, but clean and pleasant. It has a strange pricing system: 42 fl per person, with no discount for doubles.

Quentin Hotel: 89 Leidsekade, 1017 PN. Tel. 26 21 87. In the range of the budget hotels, but unique among them. Situated on a wide and shady canal, just down the street from the Maas, the hotel caters especially to artists and performers. It is located very near a small theater and the Leidseplein. Very quaint and well-kept, it has a pretty sitting area by the office counter and a garden. It must be the only hotel in Amsterdam serving breakfast till 2pm! Singles start at 50 fl, and doubles at 80 fl.

Youth Accommodation

Amsterdam is a very popular spot among young backpackers, especially during the summer. There are, therefore, numerous dormitory type facilities in the city, and some of the lower scale budget hotels have rooms for two, three or even four at a set price. The accommodation is simple, though some places also have bars or centers where it is pleasant to sit around and meet fellow travelers.

Behind the Centraal Station, there is a line of boat hotels. Most of these are geared toward youth, and prices start at about 20 fl per night. They are often the site of rowdy party scenes, and a number of them are unregistered. The level of facilities may be uneven, and the accommodation should be checked before payment.

Young backpackers may be approached by 'runners' in the Centraal Station who are seeking guests for the boat hotels and other youth facilities. Most of these people are legitimate, working for a commission and for a place to sleep for themselves.

For many of the cheaper, dorm-like accommodations, guests must bring their own sleeping bags. In some sheets can be rented, while in the cheap youth hotels sheets are usually provided.

Youth Hostels

The Netherlands branch of the Youth Hostel Association (YHA) is called the Nederlandse Jeugdherberg (NJHC). It runs about 50 hostels in the country which are part of the YHA network.

For a listing of hostels nation-wide, contact the NJHC office at 4 Prof. Tulpplein, 1018 GX Amsterdam. Tel. 26 44 33. Most of the hostels are open year-round to holders of an international youth hostel card. These are available through the national youth hostel organizations of each country. Most youth hostel groups have no age limit.

There are two Youth Hostel Association youth hostels in Amsterdam.

Stadsdoelen: 97 Kloveniersburgwal. Tel. 24 68 32. Open between March and November.

Vondelpark: 5 Zandpad. Tel. 83 17 44. A huge facility near the Vondelpark, costing about 18 fl.

Dorms

Sleep-in Mauritskade: 1 Korte's-Gravensandestraat. Tel. 94 74 44. A non-profit organization run by the municipality. 12.50 fl a night, 3.50 for extra sheets (2.50 if more than one night). You can buy breakfast at the bar and there's a restaurant with cheap meals (12.50 fl). Hostel is only open from the last weekend in June till the first weekend of September. Takes organized bookings from groups of 20 or more people for rest of the year. Bus 22, nightbus 76, from 3, 6, 9, 10, 14. Metro Weesperplein.

Tourist Information

When planning your trip to Holland from abroad, there are several valuable sources of information. In most major cities in Europe, and in several major cities in North America, there are branches of the Netherlands Board of Tourism. Information packets can be requested by phone or mail. These offices offer the Holland Leisure Card, for about $30 (see 'Discount Cards').

British Isles: 25-28 Buckingham Gate, London SW 1E 6LD. Tel. (01) 630-0451.
U.S.A.: 355 Lexington Ave., 21st Floor, New York, NY 10017. Tel. (212) 370-7367; 225 N. Michigan Ave., Suite 326, Chicago, IL 60601. Tel. (312) 819-0300; 605 Market St., Room 401, San Francisco, CA 94105, Tel. (415) 543-6772.
Canada: 25 Adelaide St. East, Suite 710, Toronto, Ont. M5C 1YC. Tel. (416) 363-1577.
Australia: 5 Elizabeth St., Suite 302, Sydney, NSW 2000, Tel. (02) 276921.

The main source for tourist information, in Amsterdam and around the country, is the VVV (pronounced vay vay vay). The VVV is not a government office, though it works with the government tourism office. It is a private organization that charges for its hotel booking services and some of its material. Nevertheless, it offers piles of information, and much of it free. The VVV can supply information on bicycle excursion routes, walking tours, rentals of bungalows, youth hostel listings, baby-sitting services, etc. The VVV also runs a program in which tourists can meet local families.

In Amsterdam there are two offices. The main one is at the Stationsplein, near the exit. It is extremely crowded in summer.

The office at the Leidseplein, where it meets the Leidsestraat, is much smaller and sometimes has less printed material, but it is also less crowded. It is also possible to write to the main VVV office for packets of information.

VVV Stationsplein office: 10 Stationsplein. From Easter till June, and September, daily 9am-9pm; July and August, 9am-11pm. From October till Easter, Mon.-Sat. 9am-6pm, Sun. 10am-1pm, 2-5pm. For telephone information, Tel. 26 64 44, Mon.-Sat. 9am-5pm.

VVV Leidseplein office, 106 Leidsestraat. From Easter through September, daily 9am-10:30pm; October to Easter, Mon.-Fri. 10:30am-8.30pm, Sun. 10:30am-5.30pm.

For Correspondence: VVV Tourist Information, PO Box 3901, 1001 AS Amsterdam, Tel. 551 25 12.

The Amsterdam Uitburo (AUB) handles tickets for an enormous variety of cultural and artistic events in Amsterdam. The publication, *Uitkrant* has detailed weekly lists, all in Dutch. But they can sometimes be deciphered, and clerks in the main office, at the Civic Theater, will be able to supply information in English. Tickets purchased through the AUB may be paid for by credit card. (26 Leidseplein. Open Mon.-Sat. 10am-6pm. Tel. 21 12 11.)

INTRODUCTION

Language

The official language of the Netherlands is Dutch. It is a difficult language for an outsider to casually pick up, and some of the place names you'll see on your map will seem incredibly long, complicated and jarring to the unaccustomed ear. It is easy, however, to find an English speaker.

Unless you are a whiz at languages, you might be better off limiting yourself to the simplest two — or three-word phrases, and relying on English. Some extremely simple pronunciation rules to remember may help you:
— G by itself is usually pronounced as a gutteral H.
— OO (*broodje*) is pronounced oh.
— EE (as in *steeg*, meaning alley) is pronounced ai.
— J is pronounced Y (*ja*, meaning yes, becomes ya).
— J besides a K (as in Rijksmuseum) is silent.
— UI (as in *huis*, house) is pronounced ow.

Yes	*Ja*	(yah)
No	*Nee*	(nay)
Please	*Alstublieft*	(ah-stoo-bleeft)
Thank you	*Dank U*	(danhk-oo)
How are you?	*Hoe gaat het met u?*	(hoo-haht-ut-met-oo)
Very well	*Uitstekend*	(out-stayk-end)
Hello	*Dag*	(dah)
Good morning	*Goedenmorgen*	(hoo-dun-mor-hen)
Excuse me	*Pardon*	(Par-dawn)

Practical tips for getting around

Business Hours

Most **shops** are open Mon.-Fri., 8:30 or 9am-5:30 or 6pm; on Sat. they may close at 4 or 5pm. Some shops close for lunch, and many will close for one morning, afternoon or whole day per week. Certain shops have late-night shopping on Thursday and Friday evenings.

Banks are open from Mon.-Fri., 9am-4 or 5pm. Sometimes they are open on the late-night shopping evenings.

Money exchange bureaus (GWK) are generally open from Mon.-Sat., times varying according to office. Some are open in the evening and on Sunday.

Post offices are open Mon.-Fri. from 8:30am-5pm. Many are open on Sat. from 8:30am-noon.

Communications

Post Office
The main post office is at 182 Nieuwezijds Voorburgwal. (Open Mon.-Fri. 8:30am-6pm, Thurs. 8:30am-8:30pm, Sat. 9am-noon. Tel. 020-5 55 89 11.) This is a beautiful structure, and from the outside it more closely resembles a church than a post office. Mail can be received here if labeled *poste restante*. Be sure to bring along identification if picking something up. Stamps can be bought in almost any souvenir shop. Mail boxes in Amsterdam have two slots. One is labeled 'Amsterdam' and the other *'Overige Bestemmingen'* (other destinations).

Phones
International phone calls can be made from the Telehouse, 46/48 Raadhuisstraat. They are placed from private booths and telexes can also be sent. Telexes cost 1 fl per word plus a standard charge of 9 fl. Telephone rates are tallied according to the country. Collect calls can also be placed. Telehouse also has several public phones and is open 24 hours a day, every day. Tel. 74 36 54.

International calls made from hotels or *pensions* cost more. For an operator-assisted call, not made from a public telephone, call 0010.

Local calls from public phones start at 25 cents, and are priced by time. Public phones are sometimes hard to find and may have lines of people waiting. International calls can be made from public phone booths, but fill your pockets with coins. For more information, call 0018. For general inquiries, dial 008. The area code for Amsterdam is 020.

Currency and exchange
The Dutch currency is the guilder, sometimes called the guilden (and pronounced with a gutteral 'h' in place of the g). More rarely, it is called the florin. The abbreviation is fl. or Dfl. Guilders are divided into 100 cents, represented by 5, 10 and 25 cent coins. There are also 2.5 and 1-guilder coins. Paper notes include 5, 10, 25, 50, 100, 250 and 1000 guilders.

Foreign currency and traveler's checks can be changed at airports, main railway stations, border exchange offices, banks, American Express and Thomas Cook. Traveler's checks are often not cashed in stores and restaurants. They can be cashed in all banks, in the private exchange counters and also, though for a worse rate, in hotels and *pensions*.

In Amsterdam, there are numerous private money-changing services, especially along the Leidsestraat between the

Leidseplein and the Kalverstraat. Money-changing is considered a free-market commercial service, so companies can charge what they want. There are differences between private changes and the banks. Be cautious, though, as often a huge service charge, or percentage, is included, and you end up with less cash than you would by going to a commercial bank with a lower exchange rate. Try to avoid all these commercial money-changers, unless in an emergency. Particularly avoid the Holland Intercontinental Change Service which adds on a ridiculously high commission. Some of the banks, charge a flat fee in guilders (about 3 fl.) for every traveler's check cashed, whatever the denomination.

American Express is a good solution for changing money. Their offices are widespread, and have long hours and they will accept any traveler's checks, not just their own, in any currency (except for Indian rupees). No fees are added on and you receive the standard going bank rate. To its check holders and credit-card holders, American Express offers additional services as well, such as using an American Express office to receive mail. The company's travel service will, free of charge, handle such arrangements as a reconfirmation of airline tickets, re-routing, hotel reservations, etc. Those who have lost or been robbed of their American Express Traveler's Checks are likely to find the local office extremely punctual and helpful in replacing the checks and handling any complications or resulting problems.

The *GWK* bureaux de change form a nation-wide chain that handle numerous foreign currencies at border posts, train stations, checkpoints, etc. It is also possible to change money in a number of international trains.

Credit Cards
In the Netherlands most internationally recognized credit cards can be used in restaurants, hotels, car rental agencies, etc. At the Dutch offices of these companies, or at various bank and currency exchange offices, credit cards can be used to withdraw money.

American Express: 66 Damrak. Tel. 26 20 42. Open Mon.-Sat. 9:am-5pm; Sun. 11am-4pm.
American Express: Koningsplein (between Leidsestraat and Heiligeweg). Open Mon.-Fri. 9am-5pm, Sat. 9am-noon.
GKW bureaux de change: Centraal Station. Tel. 22 13 24. Open 24 hours a day from Monday till Sunday.
Thomas Cook Exchange Office: 23-25 Dam. Tel. 25 09 22. Open 7 days a week; 31a Leidseplein. Tel. 26 70 00. Open 7 days a week.
Diners Club: 14f Amstel. Tel. 26 77 18.

*I*NTRODUCTION

Eurocard (Master Card, Access Card), Holland Office: 7 Damrak. Tel. 22 25 50.

Discount Cards

The Holland Leisure Card, offered to non-residents and usually obtainable outside the country, entitles the holder to substantial discounts on public transportation, admission fees to attractions, car rental, etc. Cost may change, but as of this writing it costs about $30. It is available from the Netherlands Board of Tourism.

The best purchase you can make, if you intend to be in Amsterdam for more than a day, is a Museumcard. It is available from the VVV offices for 25 fl, 12.50 fl for those under age 26. This card allows free entry to state and municipal museums, and substantial discounts at others. It is good for the entire country and is a worthwhile investment. If you visit just three or four museums you have just about made up the price, and this is a city and country of superb museums.

For those age 25 or under the Cultureel Jongeren Paspoort (or CJP) is available for about 15 fl. It includes a Museumcard, membership to the *Melkweg* center, and discounts on various theater and concert tickets. It can be purchased in the AUB at the Civic Theater.

International Student Cards entitle the holder to some sizable discounts in transportation, entry fees, etc. Some proof of current valid registration as a full-time student is necessary. The student activity offices at most colleges can provide information on acquiring these cards.

Personal security

Amsterdammers are generally very friendly and open. It is not unusual for a stranger to speak to you on the street or in a cafe; when sitting in a bar, it is often possible to start a casual conversation with your neighbor. Knowledge of English is widespread, and people are more than willing to speak it and help a foreigner. However, there is another side to the city as well.

It is advisable to keep your valuables — money, passport, etc. — in a money belt around your waist, or in a buttoned pocket, or in some other inaccessible place. The pickpockets

Dutch traditions linger on

INTRODUCTION

in Amsterdam are pros. They can cut the straps of a bag or slip a wallet from a pocket in a flash. They often work in teams, and tourists are their principal prey.

You should also beware of dark sidestreets, especially in the red-light district at night. This is the neighborhood where the addicts and muggers hang out. According to the locals these streets are growing less safe at night. Fortunately there are plenty of wide, well-lit and busy streets in Amsterdam, which are safe even in the small hours of the morning.

Drugs

In Amsterdam, marijuana and hashish are known as 'soft drugs'. Soft drugs are plentiful, cheap and quasi-legal.

The legal status of soft-drug peddling and smoking is tangled and unclear. Although not legal, soft drugs are tolerated by the government. The law defines possesion of 30 grams or less of hashish or marijuana as a misdemeanor, but the authorities seem to ignore such minor offences.

In general, do not purchase any drugs on the street. Several cafes offer marijuana and hashish menus in addition to their coffee and cake menus; any cafe with a marijuana-leaf insignia on its window is clearly advertising its merchandise, which can be smoked on the premises. Since some cafes and coffee shops do not deal in marijuana and may be actively opposed to it, use your discretion before requesting the 'alternative menu'.

In the last few years, literally hundreds of such coffee shops have sprung up. Many are found on the Damstraat and on the side streets near the red-light district. More relaxing and inviting are the small shops on the Haarlmmerstraat, just west of the Centraal Station. There are more scattered in the alleys of the Kalverstraat and Nieuwendijk. A few can also be found along the canals between the Leidseplein and the Rembrandtsplein. In the area around the Albert Cuypmarkt, there are many small shops, some of which are threatening, some inviting, but none are touristy.

There are other sides to the drug scene. The drug business is immense, and sharp operators are making bundles of money. At any time of the day or night you can find people, some quite young, getting stoned. The red-light district has quite a few seriously addicted, wasted people drifting about. Many of the people who really lose control, it seems, are foreigners who have been eagerly awaiting this freedom and accessibility to drugs.

English Language Publications

The VVV puts out a weekly pamphlet called *Amsterdam This Week*. It is filled with advertisements, but has some useful information as well, including the schedules of cinemas, theaters, concerts and special events. The *Uitkrant*, published by the AUB, includes a complete list of everything happening in the city, but it is in Dutch. The yearly *Use-It* magazine provides tourist information for youths; it is printed in English, as well as in German, Italian, French, Spanish and Dutch, and is free. It is an excellent source for bars, coffee shops, live music, cheap accomodations, etc. It can be picked up in youth hostels, student hotels, the VVV and some bars. KLM also publishes various glossy brochures and magazines.

A number of good books are available which give a general historical, architectural and cultural background to Amsterdam, and to the Netherlands as a whole. Some of the books listed here are stocked in most good bookstores, while others will be easier to find once in Amsterdam.

The Embarrassment of Riches: by Simon Schama, (Alfred A. Knopf, New York 1981). A lively, engrossing and lavishly illustrated survey of the Dutch culture and people during the Golden Age of the 17th century.

A Short History of Amsterdam: by Dedalo Carasso, (Amsterdam Historical Museum). Written by a curator of the Amsterdam Historical Museum, published by and available at the museum, this is an excellent introduction to the city for the interested visitor. Very informative and detailed, sometimes subtly humorous, and willing to confront the negative in Amsterdam society.

A Guide to Jewish Amsterdam: by Jan Stoutenbeek and Paul Vigeveno, (Jewish Historical Museum/ De Haan 1985). Walking tours and excursions cover every sign and remnant of the lively Jewish world that thrived here up to World War II, as well as spots and institutions of the renewed Jewish community. The introduction paints a detailed and painful portrait of the rise and fall of Jewish life in Amsterdam, and reveals some aspects not mentioned in most general historical descriptions. Available at many bookstores in the city, and at the Jewish Historical Museum.

The Story of Amsterdam: by Anthony Vanderheyden, (Canal House Publishers, Amsterdam/Roodveldt Boeken, Amsterdam, 1987). This colorful book in coffee-table format is too large to carry around, but is filled with beautiful photographs and equally rich, detailed prose with the emphasis on architecture.

An Introduction to Rembrandt: by Kenneth Clark, (Readers Union, Newton Abbot, Devon, 1978). The well-known art critic

AMSTERDAM

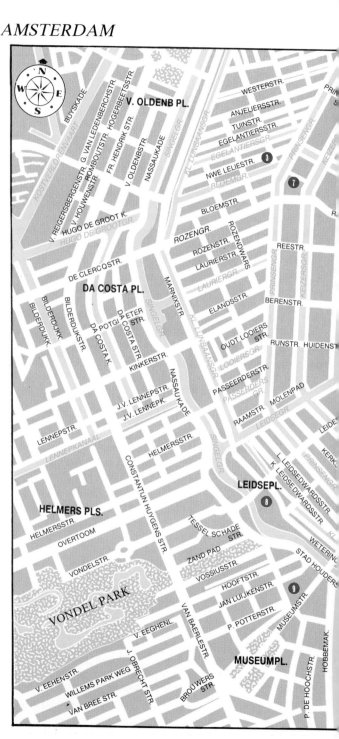

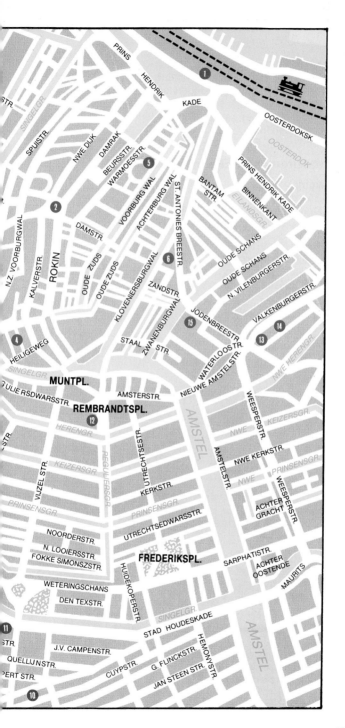

offers witty, evocative, provocative analyses of Rembrandt's paintings that make them understandable and more appreciable to the layman. Clark explores Rembrandt's accomplishments, vision, and human frailties and mysteries with much sensitivity and perception.

Measurements, Electricity and Time

Weight:
28.35 grams — 1 ounce
453 grams — 1 pound
1 kilogram — 2.2 pounds

Volume:
0.47 liters — 1 pint
1 liter — approximately 1 quart
3.79 liters — 1 gallon

Distance:
2.54 centimeters — 1 inch
30.5 centimeters — 1 foot
1 meter — approximately 1 yard
1.6 kilometers — 1 mile

Electricity
The electric power grid in the Netherlands operates at 220 volts.

Time
The entire Netherlands is in the Central European time zone. The time is GMT +1. During the summer months, the clocks are put forward by one hour.

Index

A<u>MSTRDAM</u>

Getting to Know the City

Sightseeing Tours

The VVV has a list of companies offering commercial bus tours of Amsterdam. The Touristram is a popular choice. Tours tend to be slick, but are good for an overall view. Tours depart from the VVV office at the Centraal Station. Tickets cost 7.50 fl, less for children, and are available at the GVB information office at the Centraal Station or the VVV. For information, Tel. 25 64 64 or Tel. 22 21 81.

Sightseeing Boats

The Museumboat is run in conjunction with Touristram. The boat plies the canals between the various museums on a set schedule all day, allowing one to visit a museum and then catch the boat to the next museum. There is a reduction on admission fees. Some guiding is included, but it's not a recommended way to really enjoy each museum. Other cruises emphasize Amsterdam architecture, Rembrandt, etc. Like the Touristram, these run mostly during the summer. The Museumboat costs 5 fl with a discount for children. A combined Museumboat and Touristram ticket costs 10 fl. For Museumboat information, Tel. 25 64 64 or Tel. 22 21 81.

Canal Cruises

No trip to Amsterdam would be complete without a trip on her canals. The city looks very different from the canals, which give a clear view of the building facades and rooftops. A number of companies offer canal boat rides, with many variations in theme. The basic ride lasts an hour, through the canals and into the harbor of the IJ, which gives one a beautiful perspective of the city. The multi-lingual explanations, whether by tape or guide, can be superficial, but the ride itself is enjoyable and pretty. You go under old rundown brick bridges — one on the Singel actually contained a prison at the level of the water. The Westerkerk steeple and old defense towers look suddenly very high from the water. Most of the cruise companies also offer night cruises, which have a totally different ambience. What is lost in architectural detail is compensated for in the beautiful views of lights, the reflections on water, and, in the summer, the towers and bridges strung with lights. They may be more expensive, and include wine and snacks by candlelight. Others are fullblown dinner cruises, which tend to be overpriced. Basic one-hour cruises cost about 10 fl. Some last for 90 minutes. Discounts for seniors and children.

Tickets are available at the company offices, or at the VVV offices.

Canal Cruise Companies

Rederij D'Amstel: opp. Heineken Brewery, Nicolaas Witsenkade, Tel. 26 56 36.

Holland International: opp. Centraal Station, Prins Hendrikkade, Tel. 22 77 88. The biggest company, which tends to be a bit more expensive.

Rederij P. Kooy B.V: Rokin near Spui, Tel. 23 38 10/23 41 86. It's slightly less expensive than the other companies.

Rederij Lovers B.V.: Prins Hendrikkade opp. 25-27, Tel. 22 21/25 93 23.

Meyers Rondvaarten: Damrak, quays 4-5, Tel. 23 42 08.

Rederij Noord-Zuid: Stadhouderskade 25; opp. Parkhotel, Tel. 79 13 70.

Rederij Plas C.V.: Damrak, quays 1-3, Tel. 24 54 06/22 60 96.

Pedal Boats

The canal pedal boats are the most novel way to view Amsterdam from the water. The pedal boat obviously has no guide. You are on your own to explore the canals, guided by a booklet which lists routes and interesting sights. Two companies handle pedal boat rentals: Roell and Canal Bike. Canal Bike has five moorings. Roell's mooring is near the *Amstel Hotel* on the Mauritskade. The advantage of Canal Bike is that it is possible to shove off at one mooring and dock at another. Your boat ride then becomes part of a large tour. We recommend the smaller, narrower, less-traveled channels of the old Jordaan neighborhood, near the Westerkerk and Anne Frankhuis. Roell also rents motorboats and 'family boats' with a skipper, at much higher rates, of course. At both companies, the pedal boat rentals cost about

Sightseeing by pedal boats

16 fl per hour for a two-person boat. Roell takes a deposit of 75 fl and Canal Bike takes one of 50 fl. The boats do not operate during the winter. At no time are they allowed into the harbor area.

Roell: 1 Mauritskade (at *Amstel Hotel*). Tel. 92 91 24. Trams 3, 6, 7, 10.

Canal Bike: moorings at Anne Frankhuis; Keizersgracht at Leidsestraat; opp. Rijksmuseum; Leidsebosje near Leidseplein; Centraal Station. Tel. 26 55 74.

Amsterdam Area by Area

If you are one of those who really likes to walk, then Amsterdam is the perfect place to visit.

It is very easy to walk from one point of interest to the next, in any order. Most of the major tourist sights are found in the condensed, central area, the Centrum. A few are, of course further afield such as the Museumplein, the Vondelpark and the Tropenmuseum, but even these are easily accessible by foot and certainly by tram or bus.

The focal points of our explorations in the city center include the Stationsplein, the Dam Square, the Jordan, the Leidseplein, the Rembrandtsplein, and the Jewish Quarter. Sometimes a specific route is suggested in order to lead you through a particularly interesting street, but generally you can see the sights in any order you choose.

Amsterdam is built on flat ground, recovered from swampland and sea. Due to the limited weight that a foundation in such land can support, and due to the strict building codes aimed at preserving the character of the city, there are no skyscrapers, but the church steeples reach high above the rooftops. The Westerkerk, the Oude Kerk, and Zuiderkerk provide wonderful vistas of the city, as does the Harbor Building, west of the Centraal Station. It is worthwhile visiting one of these sights first, to get an overview of the city.

The Stationsplein — Rail Hub of Holland

One's first glimpse of Amsterdam from the **Centraal Station**, especially on a bright and windy day, is a fine introduction to the city. Young people sit on the ground peddling jewelry, music is played by the ever-present street musicians. Somebody hawks a radical newspaper. Tourist boats ply the canals, and across the water you can see Amsterdam's characteristic brick gables. Old people sit patiently on benches, watching the passing scene.

The city's main information office is located at the *Noorde Zuidhollands Koffiehuis*, a venerable landmark. Nearby is the information office for public transportation. Trams and bus lines converge at the plaza. Moored in the canal in front of the plaza are the tourist canal-boats of two companies. Inside the station, information for rail travel across Europe can be obtained, and behind the station a ferry boat crosses the harbor.

If you face away from the station, and proceed straight ahead, the Damrak leads up to the Dam Square, the past and present center of the city. Parallel to it to the right, behind the first row of buildings, is the Nieuwendijk, a pedestrian shopping mall. Further to the right lies the Singel, the innermost canal, and the Haarlemmerstraat, a street of small shops and funky cafes.

Across the water to the left of the Centraal Station, behind the old squat buildings, lie the crumbling alleys and buildings of the infamous red-light district. To the immediate left are the buildings and walkways of Amsterdam's harbor and long, closed-in inlet, the IJ.

If you arrive in Amsterdam for the first time via the Centraal Station, walk across the plaza, turn around and look at the station itself. It looks more like a museum or palace than a train station, and that is not coincidental. It was completed in 1889 by P.J.H. Cuypers, the architect who designed the Rijksmuseum, and the similarity in the towers, the roofing, the inlaid stones and general motif is striking. By the late 19th century, Rotterdam had supplanted Amsterdam as the main port of the area, and the railroad began to gain importance. The nautical motifs remain, however, as can be seen at the railway station. Note the weather vane on the left hand tower, and the decorations which glorify voyages to far-away destinations. On the right hand tower, for example, the three themes of Prosperity,

AROUND THE STATIONSPLEIN

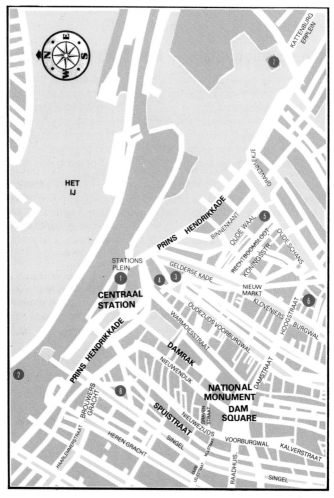

Index
1. Information Office
2. Harbor Building
3. Tower of Tears
4. Sint Nicolaas Kerk
5. Montelbaan Tower
6. Zuiderkerk
7. Maritime Museum
8. Lutheran Church

*A*MSTERDAM

Fraternity and Civilization are illustrated by two ships moored in the harbor, while goods and baskets of fish are unloaded. The station building has an especially interesting first-class waiting room in Art Nouveau style.

The northern exit of the Centraal Station leads directly out to the waterfront and a view of Amsterdam's vast harbor. The port serves about 6500 ships a year and is one of the world's largest. The huge merchant ships reach Amsterdam from the North Sea via the 19-kilometer arm of the Zuiderzee. The original harbor is seen to the right, where several artificial islands were built in the 17th century to create wharves and warehouses for the goods that flowed to and from all parts of the known world. However, the steady silting of the Zuiderzee, combined with changes in the design of ships, hindered navigation in Amsterdam's harbor, and Rotterdam's direct access to the North Sea gave it an advantage. It was only the digging of the North Sea channel which reopened Amsterdam's docks to shipping. In the distance, to the right, is the Maritime Museum.

The western part of the port is the currently the active port. To the far left of the station rises the **Havengebouw** (Harbor Building). The *Harbor Restaurant* at the top offers a fine view of the harbor. Across the IJ can be seen the tall shimmering headquarters of the Royal Dutch Shell Laboratory, with the stylized crown on its roof. Just to the left of the station exit is the **Buiksloterweg Ferry**. A trip on this ferry is a wonderful way to get a feel for Amsterdam's harbor and to catch the salty sea breezes. It's free, and leaves often.

East of the station runs the Prins Hendrikkade, a busy thoroughfare which skirts what was once the edge of the harbor. Along it are found several reminders of the city's nautical beginnings. Perhaps no more understated monument can be found than the round **Schreierstoren**, (Tower of Tears). A remant of the medieval city wall that protected the city, this was also the departure point for many shipping and exploration expeditions. A tablet from 1569 depicts a tearful farewell scene which must have been very common. From here were launched the expeditions which sailed into the unknown, such as that of Henry Hudson, who set sail in search of a short route to the East Indies, and discovered instead the Hudson Bay in Canada, and the Hudson River.

Nearby you can see the spires of the **Sint Nicolaas Kerk**, which has been a major Catholic church since the late 19th century, when the building of churches was again permitted. The gritty surroundings at the fringe of the red-light district are in sharp contrast to the sense of peace within, but, with the Oude Kerk not far away, such a juxtapositon is a long-standing part of Amsterdam's character. In keeping with the sea-faring tradition, the church is dedicated to the patron saint of sailors, who is also that of the city. On the top is the imperial crown of Maximilian, placed there after the Austrian emperor was cured of an illness after a pilgrimage here. The church had become associated with the 'Miracle of the Host', which is depicted on the high altar of Saint Nicolaas, even though the supposed site of the miracle was at the Kalverstraat.

Continue along the Prins Hendrikkade. Along this area and the canals behind it, lived some of the richest merchants and most famous seamen. Along the Binnenkant are some beautiful examples of these early houses, decorated with symbols of the sea. When you reach the Oude Schans, look to the right and you'll see the **Montelbaanstoren**. Dating back to 1512, it was built as a part of a defense system to protect the shipyards. Today it holds the office which regulates the water level in the Amsterdam canals.

Across the Oude Schans, you can see the area of Amsterdam's earliest shipyards. By the end of the 16th century, these wharves had already been incorporated as new neighborhoods in the rapidly expanding city. They later became the crowded and particularly squalid section of the Jewish Quarter. The bridge on the Prins Hendrikkade, crossing the Oude Schans, affords a beautiful view of the wide canal, the small boats moored alongside, and the Montelbaanstoren. The spire of the Zuiderkerk can be seen in the distance.

Across the bridge, at the corner of the 's-Gravenhekje, stands an impressive building dating from 1641. It first served as a warehouse and then as headquarters for the Dutch West India Company. The company had rights of trade and colonization for a vast territory in Africa and the western hemisphere, but most of its profits came from raiding the Spanish fleets, and later from a prosperous slave trade.

Further along the Prins Hendrikkade is the **Nederlands Scheepvaart Museum** (Maritime Museum) housed in a massive, low, 17th-century structure. Its origins as an armory are clearly evident. This arsenal once protected the largest mercantile fleet in the world. (1 Kattenburgerplein. Open Tues.-Sat. 10am-5pm, Sun. 1-5pm, nominal entrance fee. Museumcard valid. Tel. 26 22 55. Buses 22 and 56).

The museum is huge, with a massive collection of everything

from ship models to anchors. The displays lack a general context, as well as adequate English explanations, though a pamphlet, which can be purchased or borrowed, helps a little. Nevertheless, the paintings of Amsterdam's harbor, the huge detailed models of merchantmen and battleships, square-rigged vessels and steamers, and maps of the colonies, naval routes and early explorations do increase one's understanding of Amsterdam's rise to power. Children especially seem to enjoy the huge assortment of cannons and pistols, cutlasses and boarding axes.

As mentioned, the site of the Centraal Station itself was the mouth to the inner harbor. Where traffic now flows along the Damrak small vessels used to sail right up to the Dam and the customs office which stood on it. Today, the rows of boutiques, cafes, restaurants and shops are mostly tourist oriented, but something of the flavor of the city can be felt in the colorful crowds. There are several city maps along the way to the Dam Square.

At 34-36 Damrak there is an international newsstand. The well-known *Librairie Francaise* at No. 64 is an excellent source for books in English. In the 1930s, they published many works by German refugee authors: Bertolt Brecht, Max Brod, Stefan Zweig and others. Diagonally across the Damrak is *De Bijenkorf*, a major Amsterdam department store which was built in a neo-Romantic style at the turn of the century. *De Bijenkorf* initiated the *HEMA* chain of discount stores found throughout the city. As it had Jewish owners, the store was a scene of disturbances in the early stages of World War II, and the Wehrmacht were forbidden to shop on the first floor so as to avoid the Jewish personnel there. The Nazis overcame this inconvenience by murdering most of the Jewish employees, who numbered nearly one thousand.

At 18 Damrak, is the **Amsterdam Sex Museum** (open daily 10am-11:30pm, nominal entrance fee). Statues, graphics and various paraphernalia from the 18th and 19th century are interesting and give the place a veneer of legitimacy, but for the most part it's just another porno joint, in spite of what the management may say. Here, however, you will see couples old and young, and groups of Japanese tourists with Nikons flashing. People who would not dare patronize the little sex shops in the alleys of the red-light district, will openly browse as if walking through the Rijksmuseum, except that here they giggle a lot. Inside there is a live show in a nearby peep-show arcade, for an additional 10 fl. Be forewarned, however, that the show is

Canal near the Damrak

not in very good taste.

The **Nieuwendijk** pedestrian mall starts just west of the Stationsplein, near the Singel, and runs parallel to the Damrak, to the Dam Square. The small streets and alleys branching off the Nieuwendijk alternate between cute and crummy. The distinctive and well-known dome of the **Lutheran Church**, built in 1670, can be seen near the point where the Nieuwendijk meets the Singel. The Nieuwendijk once ran close to and along the port, past the low houses of the herring traders district. This neighborhood fell into disrepair and the church lay in decay, but it was recently acquired by the *Sonesta Hotel* to be used as a banquet and conference center, adjacent to their new branch.

At 16 Nieuwendijk is the **Dutch Arts and Crafts Center** (Open daily from Feb.-Dec., 10am-5pm, except Wednesdays in Feb., March and Nov. Tel. 24 65 01. Entrance is 5 fl.). The various workshops set up in the large basement serve mainly as a tourist attraction. Even so, it is possible here to glimpse the painstaking and highly skilled processes that go into creating the crafts for which Holland is renowned. There are glass blowers, potters, printers, diamond cutters, chinaware painters and copper-forgers.

The Gravenstraat, a tiny street off the Nieuwendijk as it approaches the Dam Square, contains some famous tiny shops. *Die Drie Fleschjes* (The Three Small Bottles) at No. 18, is a classic Amsterdam pub with a beautiful interior dating back to the 17th century. It is famous as a tasting house for Dutch *genever*. Some of the shops here, about eight meters square, may be just about the smallest in Europe. At the point where the Singel is crossed by Molstraat and Oude Leliestraat, can be seen one of the early brick bridges, the **Torensluis**. Take a good look near the water level, where you can see the window of a jail cell.

To the right of the Centraal Station, past the Nieuwendijk, begins the Haarlemmerhouttuinen, which becomes the Haarlemmerdijk, and ends at the Haarlemmerplein. It is a street of surprises with a combination of funk and style. It makes for a nice stroll, especially when all the little shops are open, of which there are a variety: junkshops, specialist bookstores, knick-knack stores, jewelry shops, and lots of little cafes, coffee shops and restaurants. There is a tremendous choice of restaurants around here. They are small, unimposing inexpensive places, and the food is usually surprisingly good. For those who want to enter coffeeshops for something other than coffee, but are apprehensive about the clientele, there are several joints along this street that have a non-threatening and even warm ambience. One famous landmark here is the *Groene Lanteerne Restaurant* at 43 Haarlemmerstraat. It is an old classic French and Dutch restaurant that must be one of the narrowest in the world. One long block away from and parallel to the Brouwersgracht, the Haarlemmerstraat is within easy access for dinner after an exploration of the Jordaan neighborhood (see 'The Jordaan — Dancing in the Street').

The Dam Square — The Heart of the City

On a bright and breezy summer day the Dam Square is packed and vibrant. A cabaret theater group plays a medley of favorite show tunes, while a would-be Bob Dylan sits nearby on a crate with his harmonica and guitar, and a nun listens attentively while sitting in the lotus position, surrounded by the pigeons that flock everywhere. An old man sells food for the birds in little one-guilder packets. Near the steps of the National Palace where the gallows once stood, a puppet show takes place, while across the square at the National Monument some African drummers are pounding out their endless, captivating beat. Part of this human tapestry are the drug dealers, the photo-snapping tourists and the punks decked out like peacocks.

The Dam Square is still the throbbing center of Amsterdam, as it has been for hundreds of years since the actual dam was built on this spot in the 13th century. This lively plaza was once all under water, until the dam was built across it, diverting the flow of the Amstel. Buildings line both shores of the river, and ships move up the newly created extension of the harbor. Today, as before, the Dam Square is the center of pomp and ceremony, business and social life. Here the Customs House was constructed, and in 1408 the Nieuwe Kerk was built, to supplement the activities of the Oude Kerk. With the Royal Palace overlooking the square, the Dam is the site where royal ceremonies are held. Here, Holland's monarchs have been crowned and have abdicated. A peace demonstration is staged on the Dam Square on the first Monday of every month.

The Dam Square serves as a central meeting point. The two main shopping malls, the Kalverstraat and the Nieuwendijk, converge here, and it is a short walk to Westerkerk, the Anna Frankhuis, and the funky old neighborhood of the Jordaan. There are streets which lead to the red-light district, and the Rokin, the main street that runs from the Dam Square, directly to the Muntplein and Rembrandtsplein. This is the point of departure for bus excursions for the city and surrounding countryside, while nearby are docks for canal-boat rides.

The Dam Square is divided in two by the intersection where the Damrak meets the Rokin. To the west looms the imposing facade of the Royal Palace. To the east stands the 22 meter high obelisk of the **Nationaal Monument**, built after World War II to commemorate the Dutch victims. It was designed by J.J.P. Oud and decorated with sculptures by J.W. Radeler. The four male figures represent the tragedies of war, the woman and child symbolize peace, and the men with the dogs are a symbol of resistence. Behind the obelisk are twelve urns, containing earth from each of the provinces of the Dutch nation, as well as from Indonesia, which was then a Dutch colony. Every May 4th, the date on which the monument was dedicated in 1956, a ceremony is held at the monument to honor the war dead and at 8pm the country comes to a halt for two minutes of silence.

Offsetting this solemnity is the crowd of young people who have made the National Monument their gathering point since 1960. People in strange get-ups just sit around, or may try to peddle various drugs to tourists. This scene unfolds in front of the elegant lobby of the *Grand Hotel Krasnapolsky*, one of Amsterdam's most dignified old hotels.

Behind the monolithic facade of the **Koninklijk Paleis** (Royal Palace) are tremendous artistic riches, created by the most famous Amsterdam artists during the 17th century. (Open daily 12:30-4pm. Ticket office closes at 3:40pm. Sept.-May, guided one-hour tours organized for individuals every Wednesday at 2pm. Admission 1.50 fl. Tel. 24 86 98, ext. 217.)

The building was designed by Jacob van Campen, with a classical exterior but magnificently furnished interior. The rooms are adorned with numerous reliefs and marble sculptures and other ornamentation. Many of the sculptures are by the Flemish sculptors Artus Quellinus and Rombout Verhulst. Two pupils of Rembrandt — Ferdinand Bol and Govert Flinck — were partly responsible for the painting of the friezes and ceilings.

It is incredible that this gigantic and expensively decorated edifice was built in 1662, not for the monarch, but merely as a functional administrative building for the city. When this town hall was completed, Amsterdam only had a population of about 50,000 people.

The unimposing facade belies the lavish and magnificent interior rooms such as the main hall upstairs. On the ground floor there is one especially beautiful and slightly eerie room: the Marble Tribunal. Here, beneath the gaze of ornately carved statues of women symbolizing the condemned, prisoners were sentenced to death. Above where the judges sat are three detailed dramatic sculptural reliefs depicting allegories of Justice, Wisdom and Law from the Bible and classical mythology. The space for the

THE HEART OF THE CITY

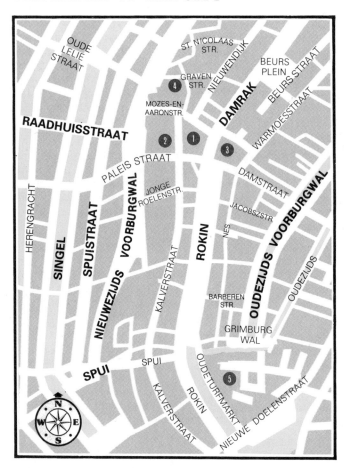

Index

At the Dam

The Royal Palace

judges' benches and the prisoners' dock are left just as they were when the hall was in active use. The condemned prisoners were brought to an upstairs room, and led out of a window to the scaffold, which stood at the front entrance, in plain sight of the crowds in the plaza. When the ringleaders of an aborted uprising against the hated 'tax farmers' were executed here, rioting broke out and the civil guard fired into the crowd.

Upstairs is the large **Civic Hall** — the lavish, breathtaking center of the complex. Note the statue of Apollo supporting the globe, and the maps of the world on the floor. These hint at the exalted view that the town fathers took of the city and its role in the world. Surrounding the main hall are slightly smaller rooms, each with a specific administrative or judicial function. There are the Finance Chamber, the Orphans Chamber, Chambers for the City Council, the Commissioners of Bankruptcy, the Directors of the Levant Trade, and a special chamber room set apart for the four powerful burgomasters at the helm of Amsterdam's governmental system.

Each room is decorated with paintings or statues that represent the role of each particular department. These works also depict scenes from Roman and Greek mythology and the Bible. They proclaim Amsterdam's role as the extension, or inheritor, of the values of the Classic civilization. The paintings and statues warned against bribes and nepotism, and emphasized honesty and justice. Some of these symbolic stone carvings are remarkably graphic, especially for a public administrative building. There are skulls and skeletons, a dog defending its dead master and, in the Bankruptcy Hall, rats gnawing at unpaid bills.

In 1806 Louis Bonaparte, Napoleon's brother, crowned himself King of the Netherlands, and in 1808 the Town Hall became his royal abode. At the end of Bonaparte's four-year reign the building went back to the city. The government could not cover the cost of its upkeep, and the new king of the Netherlands, William I, rented the Hall as his residence. In 1935 the state bought the Royal Palace and refurbished it.

Among the magnificent art works in the palace, one man's creations are conspicuous for their absence. Nowhere is there a contribution by Rembrandt. When work for the palace was being commissioned in 1655, Rembrandt was already out of grace with most of the officials and establishment powers in Amsterdam. His work was still highly acclaimed, however, and he received a commission for the Great Hall, based on a banquet in which the leader of the Dutch resistance against the Romans swore the loyalty of his lieutenants. Rembrandt emphasized the earthy character of the subjects. However, stripping a glorious national myth is not a path recommended for official acceptance, and Rembrandt's offering was rejected. Yet, in the next century, Rembrandt's *Night Watch* would hang in the hall.

On the ground floor a vivid relief map of early Amsterdam is displayed, and there is an informative 10-minute slide show. Information and guidebooks are available in the Civic Hall. The exhibits in the rooms are well organized, and concerts are sometimes presented. Check the schedule.

Adjacent to the Royal Palace stands the **Nieuwe Kerk** (New Church). (Open Mon.-Sat. 11am-4pm, Sun. noon-5pm. Nominal fee. Tel. 26 81 68.) 'New' is a relative term, since this church was built in the 15th century, and is new only in relation to the nearby Oude Kerk, built a century earlier. Nieuwe Kerk no longer has an active parish, but serves as a state historical monument, used for exhibitions, concerts and large ceremonies. It has been the Coronation Church of the Dutch monarchs since 1914, and it was here that Queen Beatrix was crowned in 1980.

The Nieuwe Kerk suffered considerable damage by fire over the centuries. In 1421, and again in 1452, it had to be restored after it was ravaged by fire. The present structure dates from about 1490.

The high vaulted interior of the church dates from the 17th century, when the church was again restored after a serious fire. The original church did not have a tower, but by the mid-17th century there were numerous calls for the building of a tower. Although the foundation was laid by driving thousands of piles into the earth, the tower was never completed because efforts were diverted to the planning and building of the Royal Palace.

The church has a particulary beautiful pulpit, a marvel of Baroque woodcarving, which is embellished with figures symbolising Faith, Hope, Charity and Justice.

Dam Square

In the church is a tomb of Admiral Michiel de Ruyter, Holland's greatest naval hero. The famous poet, Joost van den Vondel, is also buried here. Also of particular interest are the exquisite choir screens cast in bronze and the stained-glass windows depicting various national scenes.

At Christmas time, and during the summer, concerts are held, using the famous Schonat-Hagerbeer organ.

The **Allard Pierson Museum**, located on the Rokin just beyond the Dam Square, houses the archeological collection of the University of Amsterdam. (Open Tues.-Fri. 10am-5pm, Sat.-Sun. and holidays, 1-5pm. Admission 2.50 fl. Discounts to age 15. Museumcard not valid. Tel. 525 25 56.) Compared to the major archeological museums, the collection might be disappointing. The museum is small, but well laid out.

The ground floor displays collections from the ancient Near East: Mesopotamia, West Asia, Cyprus, and Egypt. The Egyptian collection is the most extensive, including some fascinating mummy masks. The upper floor focuses on the classical Greek and Roman world, including some finds from local Roman rule, and a display of finely detailed goldwork.

There are no English explanations and labels, which is a drawback when faced with case upon case of artifacts, but a guidebook in English can be purchased.

The Kalverstraat — Culture and Elegance

The Kalverstraat is a pedestrian mall which serves as one of the main shopping streets of the city. It runs between the Dam Square and the Muntplein, parallel to the Rokin.

There are several attractions either on or very close to the Kalverstraat, including the Amsterdams Historisch Museum, the adjacent Begijnhoff, the bookshops around the Spui and the Madam Tussaud Wax Museum.

The Kalverstraat was the site of Amsterdam's famous miracle. A dying man was administered his last rites by a priest, but was unable to digest the host. It was thrown into an open fire, but did not burn. A chapel was built on the spot and a road, the Heligeweg (Holy Way) was built. Pilgrims flocked from all over and they became a contributing factor to Amsterdam's growth.

Several other fantastic occurrences were reported to have occurred in the chapel. When the chapel burnt down with most of the city, in 1452, the miraculous host was once again saved. The 'Miracle of the Host' was celebrated with a yearly procession, until the Protestant Alteration of 1578. It was later revived again.

Kalverstraat gets its name from the calf trade. During the 16th century calves were driven through the street to the market which was held on the Dam.

The first shops along the Kalverstreet were the butcheries, which were soon followed by craftsmen's shops. By the middle of the 18th century over 200 shops stood here. Today the Kalverstraat is lined with gaudy boutiques, trendy clothing stores and souvenir shops. Music blares from the different shops and sometimes one can hear the oom-pah-pah of the old wooden organ at the end of the street. On busy summer days and on most Saturdays, the Kalverstraat is totally packed. This street, incidentally, has excellent shoe stores, and some have real bargains when the sales are on.

There are a few fine shops which have survived from an earlier period. Take a look, for example, at the beautiful old bakery at No. 96, with its stained glass work, and carved, deeply polished wood frames — not to mention the tempting baked goods. At No. 183 is the *Maison de Bonneterie*, which was started in the late 19th century by two Jewish traders, and quickly became a local

THE KALVERSTRAAT

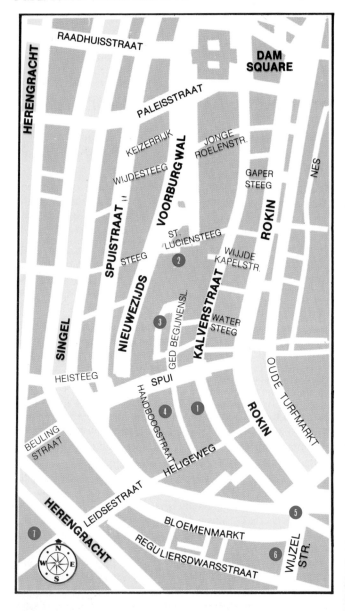

Index

institution. The classical, elegant interior, which makes superb use of space and light, has kept this store popular for all these years. The small and comfortable coffee shop here is also well known. During World War II the Nazis seized the building and used it as a warehouse for the goods of Amsterdam's Jewish textile .merchants, most of whom were killed in the Holocaust. Two plaques on the landings commemorate the company founders and some personnel, who were among the victims.

Madame Tussaud at No. 156 is a branch of the famous London wax museum. (Open daily 10am-6pm. Admission 7 fl. Tel. 22 99 49.) Some of the creations here are fascinating, and the likenesses are indeed uncanny. The front room looks like a summit conference hall for international leaders of the past: Kennedy, de Gaulle, Ben Gurion, Gandhi, etc. Further along, are displays that are hilarious in their garishness, such as the shelves with various spare heads lined up, most of them of famous people. There's Winston Churchill brooding next to Charles Bronson. It really looks like something out of an Alfred Hitchcock story, and sure enough, Hitchcock too is here! There's a merry-go-round with wax caricatures of politicians going round and round on animals, including President Reagan depicted as a giant Mickey Mouse dressed in a cowboy suit.

The entrance to the **Amsterdams Historisch Museum** (historical museum) at 92 Kalverstraat is hard to miss. (Open Tues.-Sat., 10am-5pm, Sun. and holidays 1-5pm. Admission 3.50 fl. Discounts for children. Museumcard valid. Tel. 25 58 22.) It has an ornate gate set back from the street, and is housed in the orphanage that operated here for some 400 years.

The museum has displays which document the origins and growth of Amsterdam. Exhibits chronicle the history of the city through the various stages of its expansion, including its rise as a powerful trading center and its development as a city remarkable for its religious and ethnic tolerance. The exhibits range from prehistoric finds to items of the present day. Because of the magnitude of the achievement, it is sometimes difficult to imagine how the city developed from a small fishing center to a major port with its intricate system of canals, walls and gates. The museum clearly maps out this development. Reclamation of the land from the sea is explained by means of slides. Exhibits show how enterprising builders sank hundreds or thousands of wood piles into the swampy land to serve as foundations, and how merchants transferred goods from the canals directly to the attics of their houses by winch. One of the most impressive displays is the electric map outlining the city's extensive shipping and colonial connections, spread out across the entire world.

There is a unique exhibit in the **Civic Guard Gallery**, the covered public passage, in which early paintings of Amsterdam are displayed. Although part of the museum, the gallery is a passage for pedestrians, with no charge. The collection consists mainly of group portraits of civil guards and guilds, from the dark and somber formal portraits of early Calvinists to more colorful and lively ones.

As with other Amsterdam museums, the museum has unsatisfactory English explanations, but the bookstore sells English guidebooks, as well as a brief, excellent book entitled *A Short History of Amsterdam*. There are also audio-visual programs in English and Dutch.

Take at least a look at the museum's *David and Goliath Restaurant*, off the front courtyard. The large, high-ceilinged room has been meticulously and authentically restored, with the intricate network of rafters fitted with wooden joints. Notice A.J. Vinckenbrinck's giant wooden statue of Goliath, accompanied by a miniscule David. The carving was first part of a 17th-century amusement park. Besides being beautifully detailed, the statue was constructed so that the giant's head could move.

The entrance from St. Luciensteeg passes a collection of about 20 unusual gablestones embedded in a wall. Through the Civic Guard Gallery, the public walkway heads right to the courtyard of the Begijnhof.

The **Begijnhof** (Beguine Convent) is an idyllic haven of tranquility in the heart of the bustling city. It can be reached by trams 1, 2, 4, 5, 9, 16, 24 or 25. You enter through an arched oak doorway on the Spui. The green courtyard is surrounded by elegant houses, some of which date back to the 15th century.

The court was founded in 1346 for the Beguines, members of a Dutch sisterhood who did not take vows. They lived in separate houses and retained their privacy, while devoting themselves to the ill and needy. With the Alteration of 1578, the Protestants confiscated the church at the end of the courtyard. The women were forced, like other Catholics, to continue their worship clandestinely, in improvised chapels, such as the one in the house immediately opposite the church entrance. The church had the dubious distinction of being used by the Wehrmacht. It now hosts services in English. The house next door, at No. 34, is the oldest house in all of Amsterdam, a wooden structure dating from the 15th century. Other houses in the courtyard also retain parts of their original wooden frames.

Although no longer a refuge for the Beguines, the last of whom died in 1971, the building now serves as low rental accommodation for older women who preserve the age-old tranquility of the courtyard. They can be seen sipping tea in the gardens, in an atmosphere that seems to come from a bygone world.

Near the Begijnhof, the Kalverstraat crosses the Spui (not to be confused with the Spuistraat which we reach soon). Turning west here, away from the Rokin, leads one to a small square, which is also part of the Spui. It is a very charming little area, calmer and quieter than the Kalverstraat. The buildings in the area are very old and well preserved examples of early Amsterdam architecture. Three streets — the Spui, Spuistraat and Nieuwezijds Voorburgwal — converge at this small square. Skirting this square is the Singel, which once marked the city's outer wall. Trams 1, 2, and 5, from the Leidseplein or the Dam Square and Centraal Station, stop at the Spui, right at the square.

The area is the realm of students who gather around the nearby buildings of **Amsterdam University**. There is no real campus and the buildings are scattered around the city. Along these streets, and in the alleys connecting them, are found a large concentration of second-hand and antique bookstores, pleasant coffee shops, a wide variety of restaurants, and some classic old *bruine kroegs* (brown cafes).

On the square at the Spui stands a small, mocking statue of an urchin, who became something of a symbol of the Provo movement. This area was a focal point for the demonstrations and 'happenings' that challenged the police and public sensibilities.

The *Atheneum Bookstore*, just behind the statue, is a well known and excellent source for new English books. The *Atheneum Newsstand* next door has a wide selection of magazines from around the world, including social and art journals not easily found elsewhere. Across the road from the Atheneum is the *Hoppe Cafe*, which is immensely popular with the locals. On summer evenings the throngs of students and young professionals, many in jackets and ties, spill out onto the sidewalk.

Near the corner of the Spui and the Rokin is a classic and famous bookstore, *Erasmus Bookdealer and Antiquarian*. It contains a treasure trove of books and prints dating back to the 15th and 16th century, as well as German literature and Judaica.

Night of the canals

These shops continue in the alley across the Nieuwezijds Voorburgwal toward the Kalverstraat. On this segment of the Nieuwezijds Voorburgwal are several nice bookstores and cafes (closer to the Centraal Station, this street loses its quaintness). At 9 Rosmarijnsteeg, opposite the bookstores, is a small coffee shop, *Costes*, that is a local arty hangout decorated with a stark, almost Japanese, touch. Live Japanese music is sometimes performed here. All the alleys in this area, between the Singelgracht and the Kalverstraat, from Rosmarijnsteeg up to the Spui, have a special charm, and offer a refreshing respite from the crowds and boutiques of the Kalverstraat. Some of the finest classic brown cafes are found along these streets and alleys, the kind which you enter by descending a few steps into a dark, cavern-like enclave.

If you have a taste for the macabre then head south (turn left) on Handboogstraat, after visiting the university area, until you

The colorful and fragrant flower market

are on Heligeweg, and there at no. 19 you will find the newly opened Museum of Torture, with more then 60 instruments for inflicting pain, with accompanying illustrations in English, French, German and Dutch. Afterwards head east to get back onto Kalverstraat.

The Kalverstraat ends at the Muntplein. This is really a large bridge, at the point where the Amstel River is channeled into the Singel. The one conspicuous sight here is the **Munttoren** (Mint Tower), built in 1622 by Hendrick de Keyser. It was here that one of the earliest gates into the city stood. When the armies of Louis XIV invaded Holland in 1672, the Dutch Republic transferred the state mint from French-occupied Utrecht to Amsterdam, and installed it in this tower which was part of the defense system. Today, the Munttoren houses a prestigious ceramic shop, *De Porcelyne Fles*, which sells original pieces of Delft porcelain. Lit up at night, in the summer, the tower makes an impressive sight.

The **Muntplein** is an inner-city hub where seven streets intersect and where numerous buses and trams pass. From the Centraal Station and Dam Square come trams 4, 9, 16, 24 and 25. They all continue south to the Albert Cuypmarkt, and the 16 turns toward the Vondelpark. The 9 continues to the Waterlooplein neighborhood, and the 14 crosses the Muntplein on its run from the Waterlooplein to the area of Westerkerk. Be alert when crossing the Muntplein; automobiles, buses, trams, bicycles and motorcycles seems to converge from every direction at once.

From the Muntplein stroll along the wildly colorful **floating flower market** on the Singel, with greenhouses on barges floating in the canals. In addition to an incredibly wide range of beautiful flowers, it is possible to buy bulbs and stalks of exotic tropical plants, at reasonable prices.

On the other side of the Singel; across from the flower market; is the library of the University of Amsterdam, which includes a famous library of Judaica.

The Singel leads to the Leidsestraat which can also be reached from the Kalverstraat via the Heligeweg. Although not a pedestrian mall, the Leidsestraat is a major shopping street and is usually bustling with cars and trams. The street is lined with the offices of airlines from around the world, as well as American Express and various money-changing offices.

The next street up from the Singel, the Reguliersdwarsstraat, is a strip of both gay restaurants and trendy restaurants. During the week the gay presence seems more visible, but on weekend nights crowds of young people pack the restaurants and bars here. Some are dressed to kill, lounging in joints with prices to kill!

The bridge on the Leidsestraat that crosses the Herengracht displays a map of the city for the convenience of pedestrians.

The **Bijbels Museum** (Bible Museum) at 366 Herengracht is housed in two old canal houses and is worth a visit if only for the beautiful wooden decor.(Open Tues.-Sat. 10am-5pm, Sun. and holidays 1-5pm. Nominal entrance fee. Museumcard valid. Tel. 24 79 49 or Tel. 24 24 36.) The museum itself is an unusual and lively little place, with many of the exhibits geared for children. The museum presents the Bible in visual form, as well as the surrounding cultures of the period. There are models of biblical homes, a model of Jerusalem and the Temple, idols from Egypt, and a mummy's head. There is also a collection of some beautifully printed and bound old Bibles, including rare ones dating back to the 13th century. Both Judaism and Christianity are presented and explained in a fair, balanced way. Ancient Jewish rites attached to the Temple are given especially vivid treatment.

A *MSTERDAM*

East of the Dam — Divinely Decadent

The neighborhoods immediately east of the Damrak, the Dam Square and the Rokin include some of the oldest, most charming, dangerous and colorful parts of the city. There are narrow canals shadowed by thick overhanging trees. Old dilapidated houses lean forward precariously as if about to fall into the canal. There are humorous gablestones on the wall, and old piles and winches at the water level. There are the crassly bright facades of the sex shows, little cafes tucked between them, crowded coffee shops and the smell of marijuana in the street. The oldest church in the city is also here, and there is a secret church nearby, plain on the outside but richly adorned within, and across the street are the women in the doorways of the red-light district. There is a kaleidoscope of characters: old, young, sleazy, giggling, stoned, elegant, or maybe snapping pictures because the folks back home just wouldn't believe this.

This is a fantastic area to wander around; a chance to see the seamier side of Amsterdam. At night, keep a grip on your bag, put your wallet deep in a front pocket, and stick to the main, brightly lit streets.

Worth a visit is Oude Kerk, the largest and oldest of Amsterdam's churches, easily reached by foot from Dam Square. From the National Monument, head along Warmoesstraat. One of the city's oldest commercial streets, Warmoesstraat is now much run-down, with many stores boarded up, and those remaining open include everything from sex shops and seedy bars to quaint shops run by Amsterdam old-timers. Two old coffee and tea distributors, *Geels & Co.*, No. 67, and *Wijs Koffie en Thee*, No. 102, are found along this street. The delectable aroma of coffee seems to have seeped into their walls as much as the nicotine stains of the famous brown cafes. In each, stretching back into long, old cellars, are ancient kegs, beams and iron implements.

At Engekerksteeg turn right, and follow this short alley to the wide plaza-like area surrounding the Oude Kerk. Engekerksteeg is lined with early, tilted Amsterdam houses. Take a glance at the well-known one at No. 4, with its gablestone entitled 'The Gilded Winnower'.

EAST OF THE DAM

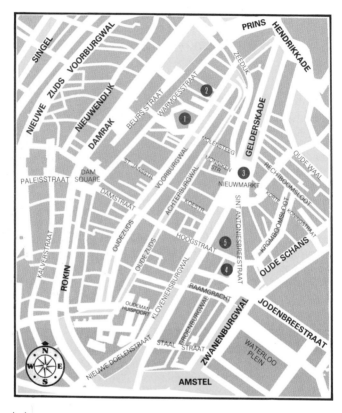

Index

Surrounding Oude Kerk are the red-lights of the prostitutes' windows. Devotion and decadence face each other as they have for hundreds of years, in this very same section of the city.

Oude Kerk is the most striking of the old Amsterdam churches. (Open Mon.-Sat., 10am-4pm, May to October. Group visits can be arranged by appointment during the winter. Entrance is 1 fl. An English guidebook is available. Tel. 24 91 83.) Its external bulk and massiveness belie the high and gracefully vaulted roof

Coffee break

visible from within. Note the intricate patterns of the beams and braces. The light pours in from tremendous height. The colorful but stylized ceiling paintings were exposed after numerous later coats had been stripped as part of extensive restorations. Taking over 20 years and completed only in 1979, the restorations renewed the resplendency of this massive church.

The church began as a small chapel built in 1306 on the site of an earlier wooden church. It's construction preceded even that of the Dam. Originally dedicated to Saint Nicolaas, the patron saint of sailers, the church was steadily enlarged, restored and modified.

The major changes, however, came with the Alteration; the Calvinists confiscated all church property when they supplanted the Roman Catholics as the ruling religious power in Amsterdam. The Calvinists disapproved of elaborate artistic works in churches, and stripped the Oude Kerk of its statues, decorations and its 38 ornate alters. Only a few reminders of the Church's Catholic and Gothic origins still remain. Along the north porch,

A *MSTERDAM*

for example, near the Engekerksteeg, note the incredibly lavish details — the balustrade, the railings and pinnacles — on this 1525 appendage. Beneath the long flagstones within the church are buried many early Amsterdam citizens, including Rembrandt's wife Saskia.

The Oude Kerk tower was the highest in the city, until surpassed by that of Westerkerk. It is still, to many, the most beautiful, with its superb detail and many embellishments. The huge carillon is considered one of the most magnificent in Holland.

The entrance to the tower is located on the west side of the church. It is open Mon. 2-5pm, Tues. 11am-2pm, Wed. 11am-2pm, Thurs. 2-5pm. If the gate is closed during visiting hours, wait awhile; the attendant may have taken up a group, and will return. Tel. 24 91 83.

Oude Kerk is in the heart of today's **red-light district**, and prostitution is a tradition as deeply rooted in Amsterdam's history as is religion. The city was, after all, a major port for trade from around the known world, and from the Dutch empire's distant colonies, people gravitated toward this center. The incredible jumble and mixture of people, not to mention sailors returning from voyages of several years, was bound to result in flourishing prostitution. The current red-light district, in the oldest part of the city, is much the same area that the prostitutes patrolled a few hundred years ago.

The district is concentrated along the Oudezijds Voorburgwal, site of the Oude Kerk, and the Oudezijds Achterburgwal which is the next parallel street. The red-lights and curtained storefronts also border the alleys which connect the two streets and branch off from them. Crowds of men window-shop for prostitutes, who sit, scantily-clad, in the windows and doorways trying to coax in clients with winks and head gestures. The women range from sexy to sagging, from to sad-looking to numbed. A large number are from immigrant minorities, and some are still teenagers.

These ladies of the night are often at their posts before noon, to catch the lunch crowd. The civic authorities regulate the trade to some degree, registering the women and giving them regular medical check-ups, with that uniquely Amsterdam tradition that balances tolerance with containment. Just as characteristically, Amsterdam prostitutes have their own organization and lobbying group.

The red-light district has become a major attraction for foreign tourists as well as Dutch visitors and Amsterdammers. The brothels, porno shops, blazing lights of the sex shows, doormen offering 'free peeks', music blaring from the bars and the addicts, peddlers, plumed punks and smirking tourists are eye-openers even for the most wordly.

On Oudezijds Voorburgwal stands the facade of an old canal house, which appears similar to all the others. The attic, which dates from the 17th century, sheltered a clandestine Catholic church, the **Amstelkring**, nicknamed 'Our Lord in the Attic'. (40 Oudezijds Voorburgwal. Open Mon.-Sat. 10am-5pm, Sunday and public holidays 1-5pm. An English pamphlet is available, and there is a guided tour upon request. Admission is 3 fl. Free with Museumcard. Tel. 24 66 04.) When Calvinist rule replaced that of the Catholics in the Alteration of 1578, the Catholics were compelled to hold their religious gatherings secretly, first in attics, barns, sheds, etc., and then in secret churches such as this one. Some were used for services well into the 19th century, at which point Catholic churches could once again be openly constructed. As in the case of the Amstelkring, the secret churches were often built in the attics above the houses of wealthy Catholic merchants or businessmen.

The attics above three adjoining houses were connected to form one chapel, the length and detailed beauty of which cannot be discerned from the outside. As with other such churches, the secret was more or less an open one. After all, large groups of people could not casually climb the stairs to an attic every Sunday morning without the knowledge of the locals. Thus the practice of the Catholic religion, kept unobtrusive, was quietly accepted.

In contrast to the surrounding area, there is a sense of peace here. The small complex was lovingly decorated and has been carefully preserved. Connecting the various sections of the house with the church are narrow spiral staircases, some of which still have the original stairs. The chapel contains all the artistic opulence that had graced much larger Catholic churches before the 1578 Alteration. Eventually it acquired a beautiful organ and a lavish alter bordered by marble pillars. The lower floors of the house have been preserved with 18th-century furnishings.

This neighborhood extends east beyond the red-light district to the Zeedijk, and is bordered on the south by the Damstraat. The Damstraat, the main street heading east from the Dam Square, reaches the Kloveniersburgwal very near the plaza known as **Nieuwmarkt**. Buses 22 and 25 also reach here.

The squat, red-brick polygonal and towered mass in the square is the **Waag**, or Weigh House. It was originally an eastern gate to the city and part of the city's defense system, dating back, as an inscription shows, to 1488. The Waag also housed various craft guilds: bricklayers, artists, blacksmiths and surgeons. So great was the hostility between the guilds, that each had its own entrance. In this building Rembrandt painted his two famous group portraits of anatomy lessons: *Doctor Tulp's Anatomy Lesson*, now in the Mauritshuis museum, The Hague, and *Doctor Deijman's Anatomy Lesson*, in the Rijksmuseum.

The Nieuwmarkt plaza is still a lively gathering point, especially on weekends. Every Sunday from May to September, an antique market is held here.

During the 17th and 18th centuries there really used to be a market on Nieuwmarkt, with stalls selling cheese, fish, herbs and cloth. Much later, during the Second World War, it served as another type of market — a flourishing black one.

Streets lead off in several directions from the Nieuwmarkt square. The Zeedijk skirts the red-light district in a long loop, back to the Warmoesstraat.

Originally part of the eastern defense system, the **Zeedijk** (sea dike) later became a center for the Chinese community. It is lined with Chinese restaurants, and a few Chinese grocery and souvenir shops, but this is no bustling Chinese quarter. The Chinese community is small and inconspicuous, and keeps itself apart. All sorts of people meander along the run-down Zeedijk, from junkies and dealers, to tourists and a regular contingent of police. It's advisable to stay away after dark.

From the Nieuwmarkt Square, one can follow the Sint Antoniesbreestraat through the neighborhood of Nieuwmarkt itself, to the Oude Schans and a bridge leading to the Rembrandthuis and the old Jewish section.

The quiet inner-city neighborhood of Nieuwmarkt, where old and new buildings meet in sharp contrast, witnessed an intense, emotional and sometimes violent struggle over the building of the underground. The construction of the subway would necessitate the demolition of the neighborhood, which is the oldest in the city. The neighborhood, once inhabited by dockworkers, was now filled mainly with young people who had an increased social and political awareness. They opposed not only the underground plan itself, but a larger planning concept which viewed the inner city as a place to work and then leave, rather than the home of thriving urban neighborhoods. For months, police and bulldozers fought thousands of young residents and their supporters, who staged sit-ins in condemned properties which they refused to vacate.

Buildings were eventually demolished, and the underground was finally built, but the neighborhood retained its basic structure and character. Along the main streets — the Sint Antoniesbreestraat, Hoogstraat and Raamgracht — one can see gaudy modular units of glass and steel backed by run-down brick walls fringed with moss.

The contrast is especially clear near the **Zuiderkerk**, which was built in 1603 by the famous architect Hendrick de Keyser, and which is now surrounded by an elegant housing project. The church can be reached by walking through the Zuiderkerkhof gateway, a small arch crowned by a skull, between 130 and 132 Sint Antoniesbreestraat. Abandoned as a religious center in the 1920s, the church has been restored and is now used as a cultural center. Note the graceful, exquisitely detailed spire that de Keyser built. (The tower can be climbed from June 1 to Oct. 15. Wed. 2-5pm, Thurs. 11am-2pm, Fri. 11am-2pm, Sat. 11am-4pm.)

The Nieuwmarkt underground station itself has become a sort of monument to the struggle to preserve both the neighborhood and its history. The collage of panels includes everything from Rembrandt's *Anatomy Lesson* paintings, to pictures from the period of the Nazi occupation, when this was a mainly Jewish neighborhood. The huge iron ball above the stairs is a reminder of the effort to preserve a historical neighborhood.

East of the Nieuwmarkt square, between the Gelderskade and the Oude Schans, there are few specific sights, with the exception of the Montelbaanstoren (see 'The Stationsplein'), but it is a lovely area to stroll around. One architecturally interesting little corner can be found at Korte Koningsstraat and Kromboomsloot. Here, the narrow streets meet at a sharply cockeyed angle, so that standing under the corner building and looking up, it appears that the building's edge is like a knife blade. The adjacent thick-beamed basement shops are typical of the 17th century and earlier.

Kloveniersburgwal, a canal once bordering the medieval city center, runs south from the Nieuwmarkt square, crossing a grid of tiny old streets to the Amstel River. There are little bars and coffee shops here, and tiny old shops, such as *Jacob Hooy's Pharmacy and Herb Shop*, at No. 12, dating to 1743. Note the old wrought-iron snake dangling above the customers' heads.

At No. 29 stands one of the city's most famous houses, the

imposing **Trippenhuis**. Built by the famous Amsterdam architect Justus Vingboons in the mid-17th century, this neoclassic edifice was built for the Trip brothers, enormously wealthy iron magnates and manufacturers of cannons. In a tribute to their merchandise, the two chimneys are shaped like mortars.

The brothers were generous as well as rich, and, as the story goes, they overheard a servant say that he would be happy with a house as large as the mansion's front door. The two brothers built the servant a miniature replica of the house across the canal at No. 26. During most of the 19th century, the Trippenhuis housed the collections of the Rijksmuseum.

Further on, Kloveniersburgwal intersects with Staalstraat, another charming little street with narrow, tilted buildings, a few old bookstores, etc. Note the building, near Groenburgwal, topped by Amsterdam's coat of arms — three crosses in vertical order and the imperial crown above it. In this building, Rembrandt painted the *Staalmeesters*, the sampling officials of the Drapers' Guild, who gave him the commission when his fortunes had started falling. This group portrait became one of the masterpieces of his later period and now hangs in the Rijksmuseum.

Rembrandt lived nearby, on the Jodenbreestraat just across the Oude Schans, and must have walked these narrow streets. Across the Kloveniersburgwal from the Staalstraat, at 24 Nieuwe Doelenstraat, is the *Doelen Hotel*, in which a wall is preserved where Rembrandt sat and worked.

Connecting the Kloveniersburgwal and the Oudezijds Achterburgwal is a long sheltered passageway called **Oudemanhuispoort** (Old Man's Gate). Once part of a 17th-century residency for elderly men and women, it has for many years housed a row of small second-hand bookshops. The niches are jammed with all sorts of volumes, as are the tables pushed out in the passage. The arched gate at the Oudezijds Achterburgwal end dates from the early part of the 17th century. The narrow streets and alleys between here and the Rokin have an array of small shops and cafes. When walking here, it is easy to imagine that you have returned to an earlier century. Following Nieuwe Doelenstraat toward the Muntplein, the bridge crossing the Amstel offers a pretty view of the river as it curves towards the heart of old Amsterdam.

The Jordaan — Dancing in the Street

Impromptu open parties are not uncommon in Amsterdam, but in the Jordaan in particular one is likely to stumble upon such a happening. A pub owner will have an open house party with beer flowing, music blaring, and people dancing in the streets. This free flowing joy emanates from the artists, students, and perennial bohemians who have breathed new life into what was once a slum. In the relaxing atmosphere of these narrow streets are some of the city's best and most authentic cafes, friendly corner pubs and junk shops which are so earthy that they don't even bother with names. A wild September Festival is held here which sometimes includes a tug-of-war across a canal.

Located west of the Centraal Station, the Jordaan is bounded by the Prinsengracht, the Rozengracht, the Lijnbaansgracht and the Brouwersgracht. A visit to the adjacent Anne Frankhuis and Westerkerk, and a stroll through the Jordaan accompanied by lunch or dinner in the neighborhood can make for a pleasant half-day or even full day in Amsterdam. This is also the area in which to find unusual, slightly off-beat souvenirs — from curious old bottles to exotic spices to handwoven baskets.

Besides the main sights to be seen, **Noordermarkt**, in the Jordaan, hosts a lively flea market on Monday mornings, and a bird market on Saturday mornings.

Trams 13, 14 and 17, and buses 21 and 67, reach this area which is within walking distance from Dam Square.

One of the paddle-boat companies, *Canal Bike*, operates a mooring on the Prinsengracht right near the Anne Frankhuis; this provides an unusual and enjoyable way of reaching the area from any of the other moorings.

The Jordaan was constructed in around 1600 as a working class district, beyond the graceful symmetry of the canals, to absorb the waves of immigrants crowding the city. A glance at a map shows that in the Jordaan, the canals are more numerous; narrower; and aligned to the other main canals. These canals follow the course of early agricultural drainage ditches that ran up to the borders of the older city. Crowded into the Jordaan were poverty-stricken workers, struggling craftsmen, Huguenots and Jewish refugees. Rembrandt lived out his last years in the

THE JORDAAN

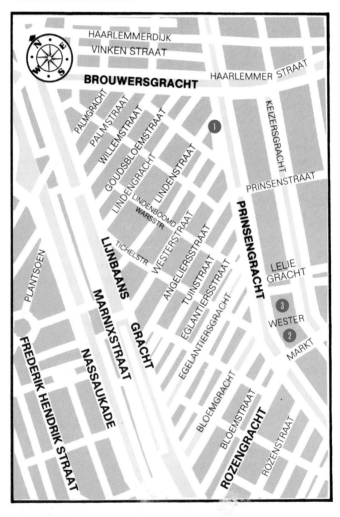

Index
1. Noordermarkt
2. Westerkerk
3. Anne Frank House

Jordaan, after being forced to give up his grand house on the Jodenbreestraat, due to bankruptcy. The streets were filthy, the quarters tiny and airless, and the canals became unsluiced open sewers. At the beginning of this century it was still a squalid slum, and during the Great Depression in the 1930s it was a hotbed for anti-government riots. Only after World War II was the neighborhood refurbished — 800 old houses were declared national monuments — and transformed into a trendy, charming neighborhood.

The construction of **Westerkerk**, at Westermarkt and Prinsengracht, was launched by the renowned Amsterdam architect and city planner, Hendrick de Keyser. He died a year after the foundation stone was laid, and the work was completed by Jacob van Campen.

Rembrandt's grave, reputed to be in Westerkerk, has never been identified with certainty. It is possible that his body was removed with others, when underground heating was installed, and it is also possible that he was never buried here at all. His son Titus, however, is buried here. Titus died as a young man, before Rembrandt himself. A small memorial stone was erected in 1909 to Rembrandt on the north side of the church, near his son's grave.

The church itself is still in active use, and is the most popular Protestant church in the Netherlands. It has a high, spacious interior, and the beautiful organ is used for recitals. When the 275 ft. tower was completed in 1631, it was the highest point in the city and remained so for many years. The tower looms impressively above the canals, the Jordaan and the low skyline of red tile roofs. Atop the tower is a replica of the crown presented to the city by the German Emperor Maximilian I in 1489. The church was the centerpiece of several paintings and is still striking today, especially when seen from the canals, unobscured by the trees. The **tower** can be visited 2-5pm on Tues., Wed., Fri., and Sat. Admission 1 fl. The view of the city from above is a fine one. If, during these hours, the tower is closed, it may be because the guide has brought one group up and has locked the gate until he returns. In the plaza at the Church stands a small statue of Anne Frank. The philosopher Descartes lived for a while at 6 Westermarkt near the church.

The **Anne Frankhuis** (Anne Frank House) is on the shady, brick-lined Prinsengracht. This is the house in which the Frank family, Jewish refugees from Frankfurt, hid with a few friends from the Nazis between 1942 and 1944. (Open June-August, Mon.-Sat. 9am-7pm, Sun. 10am-7pm. Sept.-May, Mon.-Sat. 9am-5pm,

Sun. 10am-5pm. Closed *Yom Kippur*, Christmas, New Year's Day. Entry 5 fl. Discounts for children and groups of 10 or more. Museumcard not valid. Tel. 26 45 33.)

This small, simple museum is overpowering in its starkness. Visited by about 400,000 people each year, it is one of the major attractions in Amsterdam. In summer, the line sometimes stretches along the canal. But even with crowds all around, entering the hidden doorway and climbing the narrow stairs to the secret annex made famous by Anne Frank's diary, is a chilling experience.

It is almost impossible to imagine a group of people slipping past the false bookshelf, climbing those steps to cramped, stifling attic quarters, and living for two years in constant abiding fear of exposure to the Nazis. They lived in these tiny quarters, with windows shut and shades drawn, with whispered talk, with no flushing of toilets or running of water during work hours. 'I see the world gradually being turned into a wilderness, I hear the ever-approaching thunder, which will destroy us too', wrote Anne Frank, who was a teenaged girl at the time. 'I can feel the sufferings of millions and yet, if I look up into the heavens, I think that it will all come right, that this cruelty too will end, and that peace and tranquility will return again.' She never experienced the tranquility; the Nazis and collaborating Dutch police, tipped off by an informer, burst in and marched directly to the secret staircase.

It was a very strange moment of fate and irony that when the Nazis looted the place and herded away the terrified victims, they failed to notice this diary, which ultimately had such value, and such power to condemn them. Anne Frank's death and her words became a symbol for the slaughter of 1.5 million Jewish children by the Nazis.

Accusations that the Diary is a fake and that, indeed, the entire Holocaust is a hoax, have been incorporated into the museum's ongoing exhibits on contemporary anti-Semitism and racial bigotry.

To cross the bridge over the Prinsengracht in the early days of Amsterdam was to cross into a world that contrasted sharply to the middle-class, comfortable and carefully-planned world of the inner canals. Towards Westerkerk and vicinity, the houses were well-ordered and comfortable. In the Jordaan they were narrower, squatter, and the streets slanted every which way.

At 180 Prinsengracht is the beautifully carved and polished storefront of *H. Keizjer*, coffee and tea seller and distributor since 1839. The rich aromas from this coffee lovers' paradise waft into the streets even when the store's door is closed. At No. 170 is *Rinascimento, Galleria D'arte*, featuring original Delftware and other types of hand-painted porcelain masterpieces. The old basement shop is wonderful to browse through even if you don't buy.

A little further on, across the Bloemgracht, leans a quaint little cockeyed old house. It looks as if it's about to topple, but somehow it never has. The Bloemgracht became known as the 'gentleman's canal' of the Jordaan district, because here resided and worked the more successful craftsmen. Today a few interesting little stores can be found, such as the cafe devoted to chess and running tournaments at No. 20, and the well-known bead shop at No. 38.

Walk along the Bloemgracht or cut through any of the small cross streets to the next major canal, Egelantiersgracht. It's a lot of fun to walk along these two canals, and seek out the different gablestones and coats of arms. It is interesting to note how many fascinating gablestones there are, considering this was built as a working-class area. In fact, some of the most interesting and amusing gablestones in the city were to be found in this district, a tradition that has been carried into the modern era. Although their function of identifying a household has become superfluous, the gablestones have become a traditional and integral part of Amsterdam architecture, particularly in this neighborhood. Modern versions of the old gablestones are numerous and many are humorous, ingenious or simply weird.

Along the Bloemgracht and Egelantiersgracht there are many architectural curiosities. Walk along these streets either to the end at the Lijnbaansgracht, or cut between them through the small side cross streets and alleys. On the Egelantiersgracht, be sure to stop at the courtyard of the **Sint Andrieshofje**, (if you can find it!). Look for No. 107, just beyond the corner of the Tweede Leliedwarsstraat, and stop at the three black doors — the central one is the tallest. Written on it is 107 T/M 141 C. Enter, and follow the tile-bordered passage to a beautiful little overgrown corner of the world where you can sit peacefully on a bench and almost forget the world outside. This courtyard dates back to 1616, and belonged to one of the many almshouses that graced this part of town. This was, after all, a fairly poor neighborhood, and wealthy patrons established such institutions to help the needy, of which there were many here. These *hofjes*, as they were called, were built along simple lines: a square courtyard, surrounded by tiny residences, which

Westerkerk

was entered through an inconspicuous door from the street. An administrator lived in the home, usually, with his quarters attached to the courtyard, where he could easily supervise the activities. The atmosphere of absolute, other-worldly peace you may feel here is not coincidental. It was part of the environment created with the *hofje's* construction.

At the end of the Egelantiersgracht near the Prinsengracht is another old and famous brown cafe, the *Cafe T'Smalle*. Peter Hoppe started his distillery here in 1789, and produced genever, a Dutch gin, which became famous around the country. Note the old casks and staircase, and the cosy atmosphere. On a pleasant day, patrons bring their brew to the tables on the small dock of the canal.

You'll find more small shops, restaurants, pubs and coffee-smoke shops along the narrow Tweede Tuindwarsstraat, running from the Egelantiersgracht toward the Lindengracht. One is *Burger's Patio*, a popular restaurant serving Italian food. The Tweede Tuindwarsstraat changes its name to Tweede Anjeliersdwarsstraat and then to Tichelstraat. The perpendicular Westerstraat is really a filled-in canal and also a main shopping and restaurant street of the quarter. Tichelstraat runs into a plaza at the junction with the Lijnbaansgracht and Lindengracht.

The Lijnbaansgracht, the border of the Jordaan district, is a narrow, overgrown green canal filled with small houseboats and other vessels that sit there in various states of decay but make for nice photographs. A stroll along the length of this canal is very pleasant. The Lindengracht is also a pretty canal street, sometimes livened by a market on Saturdays. The 17th-century craftsman who designed the gablestone at 57 Lindengracht must have had a lot of fun in creating that topsy-turvy world of backward names and fish swimming through trees. The Lindengracht runs into the Brouwersgracht, on which stands another famous brown cafe, *Papeineland*, one of the oldest in the city.

Nearby stands the massive **Noorderkerk**, a Roman-Catholic church built by Hendrick de Keyser in the 17th century. The adjoining square, Noordermarkt, is now the site of a weekly flea market on Monday mornings, and a bird market on Saturday mornings.

At the northern border of the Jordaan district runs the Brouwersgracht, so named because of the plethora of breweries in the area. This street was lined with decrepit brick warehouses which are now being beautifully refurbished. At various spots one can easily see the contrast between the dilapidated old warehouses and those which have already been renovated. The large central windows were used for loading docks. Now they are decorated with wide, brightly painted shutters, and the apartments are quite elegant, as an occasional peek through the windows will reveal. Brouwersgracht is also lined with canal house boats, some of which are superbly and imaginatively renovated and appear to be floating gardens.

From the Brouwersgracht, one can return by way of the Prinsengracht, or continue a few of very short blocks to the long stretch of the Haarlemmerdijk, lined with small shops and unusual small restaurants.

Along the stretch of the Prinsengracht bordering the Jordaan district, from the Brouwersgracht to the Rozengracht, are a surprising number of unique, old neighborhood bars and cafes, especially on the Jordaan side of the canal. At the junction of the Prinsengracht with the small Prinsenstraat, revelers pull their tables practically out onto the bridge. At 42 Prinsengracht is the *English Open Book Exchange.* The prices for used English paperbacks are high, and those desiring reading material will do better at the bookstores along the Spui. Next door is *Het Bruine Pard.* You can't miss the horse's head, or the carved polished wooden front with stained glass.

Stroll through the Jordaan on a Saturday, in the late morning or afternoon, when the little shops are open and the streets and the cafes are filling up. If you happen to be strolling around here on a Sunday afternoon, it is not unusual to hear singing and music drifting out from a small cafe. Because many of these small Jordaan cafes are clearly local joints you may feel distinctly uncomfortable about entering. But take a deep breath, do it anyway, and order a beer. You might be surprised at how people warm up. Swinging your glass and humming along will help, and if you happen to know the song, you're set!

The Leidseplein — Let the Good Times Roll

The Leidsestraat leads directly to the Leidseplein. At night it is easy to find: just follow the flow of the people. On summer nights things just begin to warm up at 10 o'clock. The lights start flashing everywhere and the already bustling streets and square become even more densely packed. In addition to the street performers and crowds in the street, the cafes are full. Jazz and rock flow forth. This frenetic activity continues until 3am, unless the rain ends it first. Each night the scene is completely different: new performers, spectators, backpackers and punks will take over, and a new set of chords and discords will weave above the endless rows of cafes.

The Leidseplein is served by many transportation lines: Trams 1, 2, 5, 6, 7 and 10 and buses 26, 65, 66 and 67.

The **Leidseplein** is as important a center in Amsterdam as the Dam Square, and in fact the selection of cafes and restaurants and the amount of street entertainment is far greater. The Leidseplein borders on some of the most beautiful stretches of canal — peaceful, quiet and green, just two minutes from this lively center.

The Leidseplein's role as a transportation hub and mini-carnival is possibly an outgrowth of its past when it was the site of one of the city gates where travelers left their vehicles and paid a small fee to gain entry to the city. By the 18th century the city's main theater had sprung up here, as had many small coffee houses and bars in the theater's vicinity.

At the Leidseplein itself, there are numerous tourist services. The VVV Information Booth is located on the point where the Leidsestraat meets the Leidseplein. The AUB, an extremely organized and extensive municipal booking service, has its office along the side of the Civic Theater on the Marnixstraat. Several banks and a Thomas Cook office are also located on the Leidseplein.

In addition to several first-class hotels such as the *American Hotel*, the *Mariott* and the *Barbizon*, the area has an abundance of smaller, family-run hotels in old canal houses. These generally cover all budgets, but their prime location makes them more

AROUND THE LEIDSEPLEIN

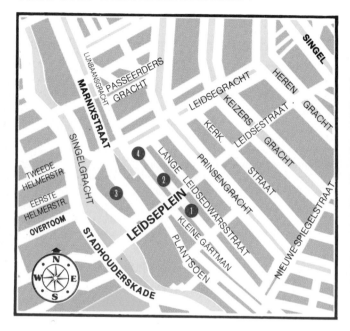

Index
1. Information Booth
2. The Civic Theater
3. The American Hotel
4. The Melkweg

expensive than equivalent hotels in more outlying areas, though there are some exceptions.

The plaza opposite the tram stop is one big terrace for outdoor tables, established with the cooperation of all the surrounding cafes and restaurants. In winter it becomes an ice skating rink. There are over 70 restaurants and 50 cafes to choose from, located on the square and several of the streets branching off from it. These include ethnic foods from all over the world, elegant first-class restaurants, as well as the fast-food outlets. There are rows of pizza parlors, one next to the other, with fancy decor and outside tables.

Rush hours at the Leidsestraat

The most striking building on the square is the ornate **Stadsschouwburg** (Civic Theater). Built in 1894, to replace an earlier theater which had burnt down, it is still in use. The theater now houses the Dutch Public Theater, National Opera and National Ballet, but these will soon be moving to the newly built Het Muziektheater (see 'The Jewish Quarter — Glimpse of a Vanished World'). The arched covered walkway in front of the building is a favorite forum for street musicians. Sometimes on a grey, drizzling morning one can suddenly hear beautiful haunting notes come floating from the walkway, clear and echoing against the background of clanging trollies and screeching tires. This is another side of Amsterdam, especially of the Leidseplein, where music will fill the morning air, reluctant to wait for the evening hours.

Next to the Stadsschouwburg, across the Marnixstraat on the Leidsekade, is another famous building, an architectural gem, the *American Hotel*. The hotel was built in 1904 by a Dutchman who had visited America and was impressed by the Art Nouveau style. Feel free to enter, look around the lobby, go up the stairs to the gallery. It has the same high ceilings, tiles, and stained-glass windows which one finds in early Los Angeles architecture, but with hints of a Mediterranean style as well. The *Cafe Americain*, listed as a national landmark, is a popular gathering place for the theater, art and literary crowds who attend the adjacent Stadsschouwburg, a tradition which goes back a long way. On sunny afternoons, the tables and the chairs are lined up outside the hotel with people who want to see and be seen.

Behind the theater is the massive brick building of the **Melkweg**, (Milky Way), a combination concert hall, theater space and soft-drug center that became a magnet for waves of wandering long-haired youth in the 60s and 70s. (334 Lijnbaansgracht, the cafe and gallery can be entered separately from the entrance at 407 Marnixstraat during the day. Admission plus membership fee, so the first visit comes to about 12 fl, after that, about 6 fl.) The Melkweg has evolved into a highly sophisticated and experimental multimedia maze. The Melkweg was the first to bring African music to Amsterdam on a large scale. There is always something new, intriguing or even bizarre going on here. Dope is part of the scene.

Across the square, at 6 Weteringschans, in a renovated church, is another 1960s 'happening' survivor, the *Paradiso*. It is even more up-scale, with bigger names and fashion shows. Admission and membership is on a par with the *Melkweg*.

There are few large tourist sights in the vicinity of the Leidseplein, but there are some pretty and quiet neighborhoods just a few steps from the rowdiness of the square. Passing through the Leidseplein to the outer Singelgracht, one can cross to the Stadhouderskade, and it is just a short walk to the Vondelpark and the Museumplein. Off the Leidsestraat, follow Lange Leidsedwarsstraat, Korte Leidsedwarsstraat, or any of the parallel streets to the east and you'll reach the line of superb antique stores along Nieuwe Spiegelstraat. This street is especially quaint and peaceful, on Sunday morning, with a few pancake houses doing a brisk business. One especially nice walk worth taking is along the Prinsengracht, from the Leidsestraat toward Westerkerk.

A MSTERDAM

The Museumplein — Art Lovers' Paradise

The Museumplein is located at the end of the strip of antique stores along Nieuwe Spiegelstraat, and across the outer Singelgracht on Marnixstraat. It contains the city's three major art museums: the Rijksmuseum, the Vincent Van Gogh Museum, and the Stedelijk Museum of Modern Art. In 1987, the smaller Overholland Museum, featuring works on paper was added. At the far end of the Museumplein stands the Concertgebouw, Amsterdam's main concert hall, famed for its beauty and acoustics. It is unlikely that a visitor will manage to tour the three major museums on one day, and it is not advisable to attempt this. There is so much to see that even the most intrepid museum-goer would not be able to absorb everything. You can easily devote a whole day just to the Rijksmuseum.

Trams reaching the Museumplein region include nos. 2, 3, 5, 6, 7, 10, 12, 16, 24 and 25.

The first museum to visit is the **Rijksmuseum**, the jewel of the Museumplein, and of all the Amsterdam museums. (42 Stadhouderskade. Open Tues.-Sat. 10am-5pm, Sun. and public holidays, 1-5pm. Museumcard valid. Tel. 73 21 21.) It is rightfully considered to be one of the finest art museums in Europe. 'Rijksmuseum' actually means 'national museum', and there are many similarly named museums throughout Holland, but there is only one real Rijksmuseum.

The Rijksmuseum was built toward the end of the 19th century, by P.J.H. Cuypers, the architect who designed the Centraal Station, and the similarities in the towers and brick overlay are apparent. Although designed specifically as a museum, the building looks as though it might have been a palace. The street from town crosses the canal and passes right under, or through, the museum itself. It's closed to cars but bicycles go humming through, and on a rainy day it's a great place to catch a free concert, as street musicians take advantage of the shelter and reverberating acoustics.

A visit to this great museum deserves to be given sufficient time. Try not to include anything else in your schedule that day. If you start to tire, take a break in the museum cafeteria. The food is a bit over-priced, but the atmosphere is pleasant and relaxing. For a snack lunch, there are some stands in front

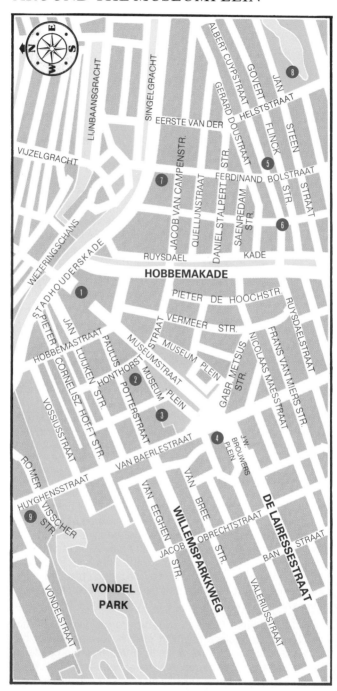

of and behind the museum (the ticket to the museum allows you to leave and re-enter, but check with the guard anyway to avoid any mix-up). With a Museumcard you can enter and leave freely.

Within its labyrinth, the Rijksmuseum holds the largest and finest collection of Dutch art in the world, from the late Middle Ages to the modern period. In addition to the famous *Night Watch* (or *The Shooting Company of Capt. Frans Banning Cocq.*) and some 20 other Rembrandt canvasses, the collection includes works by such masters as Vermeer and Jacob van Ruisdael.

There are three levels to the Rijksmuseum. Start your orientation in the central hall upstairs, where there is a bookstore and information counter. Self-guiding pamphlets and more elaborate art books are available. At various spots between the exhibition rooms one can obtain information folders which are organized by general theme rather than by room, causing one to have to jump from room to room.

From the central atrium runs a long exhibition hall, at the end of which hangs Rembrandt's *Night Watch*, the most renowned piece of work in the museum. Many people head right for it. It is best, however, to approach this canvas either through the rooms of Dutch art, to the left of the long hall, or to head slowly down the hall itself, studying the other paintings before reaching the *Night Watch*. Many early group portraits hang here.

In the room to the left of the huge canvas, various close-ups explain the painting section by section, as well as its history and the various reactions to it. In the long hall leading to the *Night Watch*, hangs one of the most intriguing of Rembrandt's many self-portraits, in which he depicted himself as St. Paul, with a turban-like hat on his head. He had been through successive personal tragedies by the time he painted this portrait, and had reached an advanced age. In its simplicity and delicacy, it is very poignant.

Twenty years prior to painting this self-portrait Rembrandt was a popular portraitist among the wealthy burghers. In 1642, the same year that his ailing wife Saskia died, Rembrandt received the commission for 'Night Watch' from a company of musketeers called the Kloveniersdoelen. This company followed a well-established Amsterdam custom of commissioning a group portrait which might somewhat glorify the stature of its members. The head of the company, Captain Frans Banning Cocq, was extremely wealthy, and the project was ambitious both in size and in theme, with everyone charging into the sunshine. The painting originally showed bright daylight, but by the 18th century the varnish had so darkened that the canvas seemed to be in shadows of night.

Contrasted to earlier dark, stiff and formal group portraits, Rembrandt's achievement becomes clear. In the immense canvas, he managed to crowd in many individual faces, each with its unique personal expression at a moment of battle. Everything and everyone is moving — seemingly in conflicting directions — yet not in chaos. On the contrary, the composition is superbly balanced and ordered, and so strong is the illusion of depth, that the two leaders seem about to walk out of the canvas.

Some art scholars claim that Rembrandt's painting roused his patron's anger because he emphasized individuality instead of unity and this initiated his fall from popular grace. Others insist that the painting was accepted, since in 1715 it was transferred to the War Council Chamber of the Town Hall (where two figures were sliced off the left edge to make it fit). In any case, there it hung for many years, a tribute to the master whose work was not admitted into the same building while he was still alive.

The maze of exhibition rooms to the left of the long central hall, exhibiting a definitive and superb collection of Dutch painting, starts with Christian scenes from the medieval period. Presented roughly in chronological order, the paintings highlight the unfolding of a wonderfully warm and colorful sense of artistic freedom, as seen in Frans Hals' portraits and van Ruisdael's pastoral landscapes. Dutch painters in the 17th century concentrated on scenes of everyday life, and in paintings by Vermeer, such as *The Kitchen Maid* and *Young Girl Reading a Letter*, these everyday moments acquire a noble and monumental character.

Foreign masters in the Rijksmuseum collection include Rubens, Goya and Van Dyck. In addition, there is an extensive collection from East Asia: porcelain from Japan, bronzes from Tibet, and paintings from Cambodia and Siam. There are large collections of dollhouses, china, tapestries, furniture, silverware, jewelry, ivory, shellwork and wood carvings. These household furnishings for the upper classes range from the intricately detailed to the incredibly tiny and delicate, and all testify to the tremendous output of fine craftsmanship in the Netherlands and northern Europe during the pre-industrial 18th century. There are also temporary exhibits and slide shows in the small auditorium. Check at the information hall for schedules. In the large exhibition rooms there are explanations of the history of the city and region. Notice the huge, mechanical clock which may mesmerize you as you try to figure out how it works.

To reach the **National Vincent Van Gogh Museum** walk down Museumstraat, turn right into Honthorststraat and left at Paulus Potterstraat. (7 Paulus Potterstraat. Open Tues.-Sat. 10am-5pm, Sun. and public holidays 1-5pm. Museumcard valid. Tel. 16 48 81).

The Van Gogh Museum, designed by Gerrit Rietveld, houses a collection of paintings, drawings, graphic art and documents by Vincent van Gogh (1853-1890), plus works by his comtemporaries, including Gauguin and Toulouse-Lautrec. The collection belonged to Vincent's brother Theo, and was passed to his wife and son, and in 1931 the collection was put on permanent display at the Stedelijk Museum. The Van Gogh Museum was opened in 1973.

The collection includes over 200 paintings and 500 drawings by Van Gogh, his original letters to his brother Theo, Japanese woodcuts (which influenced Van Gogh's style), archival material, and a shop selling slides, posters and so on. The letters to Theo reveal a great deal about Van Gogh's life and personality, and also express his ideas about life and his own paintings. Theo was Vincent's unfailing supporter, both emotionally and financially.

The halls of the beautifully designed Van Gogh Museum are open and light-filled. Surrounded by hundreds of Van Gogh canvases and drawings, including many of the most famous and familiar ones, viewers move slowly and intently, seemingly oblivious of the crowds. The presentation roughly follows Van Gogh's artistic development, from early somber peasant scenes

The Rijksmuseum

Rembrandt at his peak

to the final landscapes in which sky and fields are transformed into masses of blazing color.

Vincent Van Gogh burst into creative maturity like one of the bright sunflowers he painted. It was in 1880 that he made his full commitment to art, and in 1890 at age 37 that he shot himself. In those intervening ten years, however, Van Gogh experienced a period of remarkable creativity.

After working without much success for an art dealer, as a teacher, and as a lay preacher in a poor mining region, Van Gogh began to draw and paint. These early works are rather dark, heavy and somber.

While working in The Hague, Van Gogh became involved with a pregnant prostitute, Sien, and he drew her naked, sagging, hunched body in his moving sketch *Sorrow*. After a painful split from Sien, Van Gogh moved to the rural province of Drenthe, a world of marshland, fields and cottages. Here, after doing many sketches of peasants, Van Gogh produced a rough-hewn masterpiece, *The Potato Eaters*. The painting shows a family of peasants gathered around a table in a dark and smoky room, lit only by a single glowing lantern. Van Gogh compassionately portrays their forbearance in the face of poverty.

Van Gogh moved to Paris and stayed with his brother Theo from 1886-1888. Theo, an art dealer, knew many of the Impressionists and supported their work. Vincent, who had been seriously working for only five years, was introduced to, and largely accepted as an equal by such painters as Seurat, Toulouse-Lautrec and Gauguin. Paris and the Impressionists had great impact and a liberating effect on Van Gogh. His brush-strokes broadened and his paintings were suddenly filled with color. Two examples of his work from this period are *Pont de la Grande Jatte*, (1887) and *Woman Sitting in the Cafe du Tambourin* (1887).

Feeling the need to escape Paris after two years, Van Gogh moved to Arles in southern France, where he stayed for the next two years (1888-1890). Van Gogh, who came from the cold wet lowlands with their dense black skies, was intoxicated by the blazing sunlight, the fruit trees, the wheat fields, and the rolling hills under limpid skies. It was here that his style reached full maturity, going beyond Impressionism to create his personal style of Post-Impressionist painting. His colors became even richer, his texture thicker, and his paintings filled with light and warmth. *Vase with Sunflowers* (Jan. 1889), *Orchard in Provence* (1888) and *The Bedroom* (1888) are examples of his paintings done at Arles. These pictures are calm, composed and harmonious. He produced over two hundred paintings in about a year, plus drawings. Even the simplest objects — an onion, a pipe, his tiny room — were imbued with an internal light. But while creating these masterpieces he was deeply lonely, and he suffered from depression and emotional instability. Some of his self-portraits reflect these inner struggles, and some convey a disturbing or threatening feeling. *Crows in the Wheat Fields* (1890) is one such troubling painting, with its harshly contrasting colors, paths leading nowhere, and dark, menacing sky.

After an attack of mental instability, Van Gogh spent a year of voluntary recuperation in the asylum at Saint-Remy, where he painted the garden and his fellow patients, producing over a hundred canvases.

After briefly visting his brother in Paris, Van Gogh went to Auvers where he placed himself under the care of a doctor. Despairing of a cure, Van Gogh walked into the wheatfields with a revolver and shot himself. Theo rushed to his wounded brother, and stayed with him until he died two days later.

Virtually next door to the Van Gogh Museum stands the **Stedelijk Museum**. (13 Paulus Potterstraat. Open 11am-5pm daily. Admission 7 fl. Museumcard not valid. Tel. 573 27 37 or Tel. 573 29 11.)

The Stedelijk Museum, Amsterdam's museum of modern and contemporary art, is considered one of the three major art museums in the city. Its huge collection features mainly 19th and 20th-century painting, especially Dutch and French. There are early moderns, abstract, surrealist and conceptual painting, sculpture, photography, prints, graphics, collages, industrial design and artistic experiments utilizing video and other rapidly developing technologies.

While people stare long and intently at the compassionate paintings hanging in the Van Gogh Museum, in the Stedelijk it is common to see them rush through giant exhibit halls. There is a heavy concentration of intellectualized art, visual concepts dismantled into parts and disembodied from human emotion, and some exhibits seem pretentious.

There are, however, a few rooms with canvases by Picasso, Van Gogh, Monet, Manet, Cezanne and others, which are like a garden in a desert for those who have little sympathy with ultramodern art. Then there is a small but wonderful collection of large Chagall canvases, including his painting of a green violinist playing above the village roofs. There are about 50 paintings, gouaches and drawings by Malevich, one of the early abstractionists.

Perhaps as some artistic statement, the first floor seems to be a jumble in which restrooms, restaurant and galleries are interspersed with no seeming order. The restaurant (a bit overpriced as are most museum restaurants) looks over the sculpture garden and is a nice place to relax over a coffee.

In the basement, you'll find Kienholz's *Beanery*, a fascimile of a tiny, crammed, noisy Los Angeles bar, jammed with squat but life-like figures, which all have clocks for faces. You will be engulfed in a scene that is claustrophobic, cynical, beautifully detailed and funny.

The Stedelijk is an incredibly active museum and learning center. There is a constant flow of new and visiting exhibits. Plenty of information is available at the door, and there are programs of films (Sunday afternoons) contemporary music (on Saturdays from September to June) and various lectures and performances. There is also a library well-stocked with books, magazines and catalogs of modern art.

At 4 Museumplein you will find the **Museum Overholland**. (Open Tues.-Sat. 11am-5pm, Sun. 1-5pm. Tel. 76 62 66.) It is a new museum which is part of the Stedelijk Museum complex. It features mainly works on paper: drawings, gouaches, collages and pop posters by contemporary artists. The emphasis is on Dutch artists, but works by international artists are also exhibited.

The **Concertgebouw**, a world-famous concert hall built in the late 19th century, stands at the far end of the Museumplein, at 98. Van Baerlestraat. It is known both for its acoustics and the Concertgebouw Orchestra it hosts. Schedules and tickets are available at the AUB in the Leidseplein.

The **Albert Cuypmarkt** is a must for the sheer fun of strolling through it. This is Amsterdam at its unpretentious best. No touristy shops here, just a typical Amsterdam crowd of faces from around the world — 20,000 on a busy day — squeezing between the two rows of stalls on Albert Cuypstraat. This market is far more authentic and down to earth than the much touted Waterlooplein flea market. Here you can still find a beautiful hand-knitted sweater for next to nothing.

Vendors hawk their produce. The flower stalls are a riot of color and the cheeses are piled on wagons. Sample the olives and pickles, the pungent fish laid out in rows and the eels smoked on

Albert Cuypmarkt - a typical Amsterdam Crowd

the spot in big garbage cans. Here you'll find nut stalls, tea stalls, and mounds of fruit. The little shops behind them sell luscious local chocolates (at prices that beat the airport duty-free shops, so buy your gifts here). On the periphery of the market are some of the cheapest eateries in town, tiny Chinese and Surinamese joints serving huge steaming chicken rice specials for as little as 5 fl.

Notice how drab and uniform many of the buildings are behind the stalls. In the late 19th century, the city opened this tract of pastureland to builders who cheaply, profitably and sometimes shoddily built a working-class neighborhood to house the influx of people to the city. The buildings were soon tenanted by Jewish and foreign workers, and even then the street was filled with hundreds of market stalls. Jewish hawkers were particularly prominent but business was initially crippled during the Depression, and then further when the populace was devastated by the Nazis. Today, the 19th-century proletarian flats once again house foreign workers, but from beyond Europe, and the market, now booming, is simply carrying on a tradition.

The market starts to quiet down at about 4pm and is closed by 5pm. It's the perfect antidote for the high culture of the nearby Museumplein. A morning visit to a museum and a short visit here for lunch and a stroll make for a very pleasant day.

The main cross-street to Albert Cuypstraat is Ferdinand Bolstraat (both main streets in this working-class district were named for artists), which is a shopping street and main thoroughfare, lined with cut-rate shoe stores and clothing stores, and the usual array of homey little Amsterdam shops.

Very near the Albert Cuypmarkt stand two other solid Amsterdam institutions. A. van Moppes & Zoon Diamonds and the original Heineken Brewery.

A. van Moppes & Zoon Diamonds is located at the western end of Albert Cuypstraat, just a short walk from the market. (2-6 Albert Cuypstraat. Open weekdays 9am-5pm. Tel. 76 12 42.) Started by the son of a diamond worker, van Moppes was one of the first diamond concerns to introduce steam-powered cutting and polishing. It expanded rapidly to become the largest company in Amsterdam, with branches around the world. The business moved to Brazil during World War II and returned after it ended, moving into the current building. Ironically, this building had, during the war, housed a training school for diamond cutters and polishers run by the Nazis.

The free tour is extensive and detailed, running through the cleaving, cutting and polishing processes that create diamonds suitable for jewelry. The factors determining a diamond's quality and price are explained, and among the exhibits is the smallest cut diamond in the world, which can be viewed through a microscope. An engaging explanation of the technical processes requires excellent tour-guiding, but unfortunately the level of the guiding is uneven. After the tour, of course, there is ample opportunity to purchase diamonds.

At the corner of Ferdinand Bolstraat and Stadhouderskade stands the old brick **Heineken Brewery**, now one of several branches. Heineken is the most widely distributed and popular beer in Amsterdam. If you buy a beer on tap, it is probably Heineken. Its biggest competitor, Amstel, shares certain distributing facilities with Heineken. From a small family-owned brewery (it is still a family business), the brewery has branched out to produce soft drinks and hard liquors.

Unfortunately, this original branch closed in April 1988, but apparently you can still tour the building from 10am-1:30pm at a cost of one guilder and plans are in the works for opening a beer museum in the building. Call the main office for more information. Tel. 071-81 50 08.

Just south of the Albert Cuypmarkt, along Van Der Helststraat, is **Sarphati Park**, a peaceful spot to enjoy a picnic lunch bought at the market stalls. The brick house by the small pond looks like a village mill scene. There is a large, slightly overblown monument to Samuel Sarphati, whose efforts at planning a green area for this proletarian neighborhood resulted in this park. Actually, Sarphati had secured a much larger tract for an urban park, but after his death the turf was sold off bit by bit, at profitable rates, before this small plot was finally secured as a park.

From the Museumplein, there are several nice walks. Bear in mind that some sights are equally accessible from the Leidseplein; the two landmarks are really very close, and its only a ten minute walk from the one to the other. Almost right next door is the green and lively Vondelpark.

The **Vondelpark** is Amsterdam's main urban park. The entrance to its panhandle is on the Stadhouderskade, just across the outer Singelgracht from the Leidseplein. Named for the 17th-century poet Joost van den Vondel, who is considered to be one of Holland's greatest, the park became a favorite meeting point for the hippie invasions of the sixties and early seventies, when by day and night it was filled with wandering youths. The park has maintained that tradition, but sleeping in the park is now prohibited. A youth hostel bordering the park still provides easy access, as do small, classier hotels in the pretty, established neighborhood. Public transportation is convenient from all directions. From the center of town run trams 2, 3, 5 and 12. Starting from the Stationsplein, the 16 circles almost the entire park.

Some days the park is tranquil, but the next day the whole place may be alive with an outdoor concert, a children's play, an impromptu festival, or a football or Frisbee game possibly with the participants dressed bizarrely as circus clowns. On Sunday people pour into the park, to hear the free music of the bands.

There are many scheduled open-air rock concerts, classical concerts, and numerous other events. During the annual Holland Festival there is always something happening in the Vondelpark. Every two years, the uproarious Festival of Fools takes over. Local listings cover all these events.

The 48-hectare (120-acre) park is closed to motorized traffic. The tree-lined road skirting its borders is a favorite route for joggers and cyclists. The park, landscaped on English lines, is dotted with gardens, ponds and groves. There are snackbars, cafes and restrooms at the western and the more lively eastern end of the park.

At the western end of the park, the small tea-house is in a small paddock in which sheep and cattle graze, surrounded by moats. The rose garden is especially beautiful and relaxing. The drooping willows at the nearby stream, and the lovely arched iron bridge seem to belong in the countryside.

A pretty 19th-century building in the park houses the **Nederlands Filmmuseum**. (3 Vondelpark. Open Mon.-Fri. 10am-5pm. The library and information center are closed on Mon. Free admission. Tel. 83 16 46).

The museum collects and preserves both Dutch and international films deemed important to the study of cinematography and the development of the cinema. Films chosen according to theme are shown in the evening. Check for schedules.

In addition to a permanent exhibition on the development of cinematic technology, the museum presents temporary exhibitions. The library contains thousands of titles and hundreds of film journals.

The Rembrandtsplein — Museums and Nightlife

The **Rembrandtsplein** shares with the Leidseplein the distinction of being a main center of Amsterdam nightlife, but the entertainment here is different in character. The Rembrandtsplein tends to be quieter and more businesslike during the day, while at night it is the prime area for nightclubs, strip shows and gay clubs. It is easily reached by foot from the city center and from other main areas. Trams 4, 9, and 14 reach the square.

The center of the square is a fenced-in plot of grass in which stands a statue of Rembrandt. It was only in 1876 that the square was dedicated to that great artist. Originally, in the late 16th century, it was part of the city's ramparts and later, as the city expanded, it was used as a butter market. It later became a bustling center, especially for colorful and lively fairs. That tradition still continues in some ways. In the evening on weekends the sound of live music flows from every bar, cafe and restaurant, while under Rembrandt's statue another band will be playing. The entire square is lined with long, narrow bars, bright modern cafes with outdoor patios, and some expensive restaurants. Some of the bars, such as *Rembrandt's Bar* attract an older Dutch crowd who enjoy singing together, beer mugs swinging, along with the bartender.

Just off the Rembrandtsplein, in the direction of the Muntplein on 16-28 Reguliersbreestraat looms the **Tuschinski Theater**. The imposing building stands out among the the snack bars, pizzerias, gay bars and porno movie houses which line the street. This Art-Deco masterpiece, which is one of the most famous cinemas in the world, is harmonious in the detail both of its facade and interior. Completed in 1921, it was the obsessive creation of theatrical producer Abram Icek Tuschinski, and its construction was guided by Tuschinski every step of the way. The luxurious curtains, the handmade Persian carpets, the colored marble, and the chandeliers blend the Art-Deco design of the 20s with everything from *Arabian Nights* to a touch of *Phantom of the Opera*. Tuschinski, a Jew, was killed at Auschwitz.

Guided tours, lasting about 75 minutes, are conducted at 10:30am on Mon., Tues. and Wed. for 5 fl. During July and

AROUND REMBRANDTSPLEIN

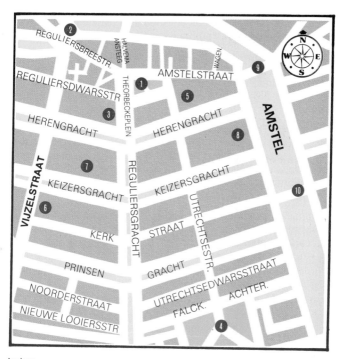

Index

August, organ concerts are held every Saturday at 11am, using the organ that accompanied early films at the cinema. Tel. 23 15 10.

Back on the square itself one can visit several famous old Amsterdam cafes, such as the *Old Bell*, a dark and comfortable place on the corner of Utrechtsestraat and the square, and the nearby *Cafe Schille*, at 26 Rembrandtsplein, a famous haunt for artists and intellectuals. On weekend nights and Sunday afternoons, gays and straights alike crowd the friendly gay bars that line the Halvemaansteeg, which is a short alley leading from the square to the Amstel River. At No. 56 stands **De Kleine**

Komedie, the oldest continually operating theater in the city, which opened at the end of the 18th century. Having undergone many diverse alterations including being used as a missionary church, it has again been established as a playhouse, featuring many English-language productions. Check the AUB for listings.

The Reguliersdwarsstraat, behind and roughly parallel to the Reguliersbreestraat, also has several fine restaurants, as well as some gay hang-outs. On the corner with the Rembrandtsplein stands the *Nightwatch*, which is famous for its steaks and shrimp.

The nearby **Theorbeckeplein** is basically an extension of the main square. Its open space and the gazebo in the center are regularly used for various festivals and fairs, of which there are an endless variety in Amsterdam. Every Sunday in the summer an open-air fair is held here, along with an arts-and-crafts market, from noon to about 6pm.

Continuing from the Theorbeckeplein, the Regulieregracht has a few small, family-run hotels, and it offers interesting views of the canal bridges. The Utrechtsestraat, at the east end of the square, is lined with small shops and many restaurants, and runs south to the Frederiksplein, which offers one a haven of shade and green, near the outer Singelgracht.

Just south of the Rembrandtsplein runs the **Herengracht**. This was Amsterdam's most elegant residential quarter in the second half of the 17th century. Along this segment of the 'gentlemen's canal' stand particularly dignified facades which bear testament to the area's illustrious past. The luxurious interiors contrast sharply with the austere exteriors. No. 527 was once inhabited by the Russian Czar Peter the Great, and No. 502 is the official residence of the mayor.

The **Willet Holthuysen Museum**, at 605 Herengracht, near the Utrechtsestraat, is a typical canal house of an eminent 17th-century burgher in Amsterdam. (Open Tues.-Sat. 10am-5pm, Sun. and holidays 1-5pm. Nominal fee. Museumcard valid. Tel. 26 42 90.)

The house has been preserved intact, down to the marble mantelpiece, painted ceilings and intricate wooden carvings. There is a short slide show in English accompanied by soothing 18th century music. The house, built in 1687, was first owned by an Amsterdam diplomat and town counselor. In 1855, it passed to Pieter Gerard Holthuysen, and then to his only daughter, who married a man named Abraham Willet. The house, impressive enough in its own right, is filled with his collections of glass, ceramics, silver and paintings. The museum is worth a visit if only to gain some insight into the domestic life of the wealthy in the early days of Amsterdam. There is a tranquil and beautifully hedged garden, which dates back to the 18th century. It is also visible from the Amstelstraat side.

Another canal house museum, the **Van Loon Museum**, is located nearby at 672 Keizersgracht. (Open Mon. 10am-5pm.) It is smaller and less well-kept, than its sister on the Herengracht, evidently due to budgetary problems. Its claim to fame, beyond the usual family history, is that the artist Ferdinand Bol lived here for some time after its completion in 1672. This house belonged for hundreds of years to the Van Loon family who purchased it shortly after it was built. In addition to the antique fixtures, furniture and other objets d'art, there is a collection of some sixty Van Loon family portraits dating from the 17th and 18th century. Visiting one of these two house museums is usually sufficient.

At 609 Keizersgracht is the **Fodormuseum**, run under the auspices of the Stedelijk Museum. (Open Tues.-Sat. 10am-5pm. Museumcard valid. Tel. 16 24 25.) It is a small museum, with rotating exhibits of work by contemporary artists, mostly from Amsterdam. Special presentations are prepared for the summer. The range of the work is great and the quality variable. A monthly magazine provides information in English.

The **Six Collectie** (Six Collection), 218 Amstel, is a private collection of 17th-century Dutch Masters, including several paintings by Rembrandt. (To enter this museum you will need a note of introduction from the Rijksmuseum. Museumcard valid. Call the Rijksmuseum for details: Tel. 73 21 21.) The *Portrait of Jan Six* by Rembrandt is the centerpiece of the collection. In broad, unfinished strokes, Rembrandt catches Jan Six's air of casual confidence. He was a wealthy and influential man and a friend and creditor of Rembrandt. Works by Frans Hals are also included in this striking selection.

Two well-known diamond works are located near the Rembrandtsplein. The *Holshuysen-Stoeltie Works*, at 13-17 Wagenstraat, include some 19th-century machines, which bear evidence to the exacting craftsmanship essential to the trade. Visitors are welcome. Tel. 23 76 01.

Amstel Diamonds, at 208 Amsteldijk, was a major company that once held a monopoly on diamond chips. It is one of the most popular of the diamond works with visitors, and includes a showroom and explanations of the diamond-production process.

Heading east from the Rembrandtsplein runs the Amstelstraat, which is today a rather depressing, slightly run-down street of discos, a few gay bars and some shwarma kiosks, selling middle-eastern style lamb roasted on a vertical spit. There is

Tranquility at the Rembrandtsplein

very little to remind you that this was once a stylish theater street, filled with promenaders and lined with cafes. Amstelstraat also formed the link between the Rembrandtsplein and the central city.

The **Blauwbrug** which connects Amstelstraat with the Jewish quarter, is named for a blue wooden bridge that no longer exists. The current bridge, built in 1883, is a copy of Pont Alexandre in Paris which spans the Seine. It is richly adorned with golden crowns and ships' prows. To the north it faces the new opera house, a sleek glass and concrete structure which stands in what was once the old Waterlooplein flea market.

To the south of the Blauwbrug, an old drawbridge spans the Amstel. This is the **Magere Brug** (Skinny Bridge), probably the most photographed bridge in the city. It is the last of the hundreds of wooden bridges that crisscrossed Amsterdam's canals. Even today two uniformed attendants raise and lower the bridge with cranks and ropes for the barges which constantly glide beneath.

Typical facade

Magere Brug at night

The Jewish Quarter — Glimpse of a Vanished World

Towards the end of the 16th century the newly created Republic of the Netherlands prohibited religious persecution. This paved the way for many Jews, and for other religious minorities who were fleeing persecution, to find refuge in the Netherlands. This factor as well as Amsterdam's rapidly expanding trade, attracted the Spanish — Sephardic — Jews, who had suffered terribly under the Spanish Inquisition.

Many of the Jews prospered as merchants, and took a visible, vibrant role in the city's economic, public and intellectual life. It was this intellectual climate that nurtured the great Jewish Dutch philosopher Baruch Spinoza. Primarily a rationalist, his independent thinking ran counter to Jewish beliefs, and led to his excommunication from the Jewish community in 1656.

Religious tolerance was, however, accompanied by severe economic restrictions. Barred from entering the guilds which controlled most trades and crafts, and forbidden to own shops, the Jews of Amsterdam were forced into the street trade. Poverty, which was rife, increased with the influx of German Jews, the Ashkenazis.

Although not forced into a ghetto, the Jews were alotted residential areas unwanted by others, such as old shipyards (the Waterlooplein was once a marshy island used for shipping). These were transformed into crowded, squalid mazes. Jewish neighborhoods spread from the Visserplein area to Nieuwmarkt, and to the south.

Civic authorities often turned a blind eye to the trade restrictions and some Jews slipped into certain guilds and succeeded in opening shops. They also established and introduced some new industries such as silk, printing, and especially diamonds, helping to later make Amsterdam the diamond center of the world.

In 1796 with the invasion of the Republican French army, the economic restrictions against Jews were abolished. The Jewish elite welcomed the chance to join the general bourgoisie, and some were even baptized. In spite of this new freedom, and the assimilation which came in its wake, many Jews remained poor up until the mid-19th century, when Holland began to develop its industrial potential.

In the 1870s the diamond industry boomed with the discovery of diamonds in South Africa. Jews played a major role in the diamond and other industries, and, consequently, in the workers' movements that swept through the industrial centers of Europe. By the turn of the century, 60,000 Jews lived in Amsterdam. They had long since broken out of the old Jewish center between the Nieuwmarkt and Meijerplein.

During the 1930s Jews fled from the rising anti-Semitism in Germany to the Netherlands. Waves of Jewish immigrants, however, put a strain on Dutch resources, which led to restrictions in immigration.

The Germans invaded in 1940. Immediately, anti-Jewish measures were imposed: Jewish travel was restricted, workers were fired, lists compiled, telephones cut off, and Jews were forced to wear the yellow star. A Jewish bank was taken over and, ironically, Jewish funds were transferred here and used to finance the deportation and extermination of the Jews.

In February 1941, some German officers were sprayed with ammonia in a small Jewish ice cream parlor. The owner was promptly arrested and executed, and the incident was used as a pretext for the first major round-up of some 400 Jews for deportation. This, in turn, led to the strike by dockworkers, initiated by the Communists, largely in support of their Jewish fellow workers. The brave but futile strike was crushed brutally in two days.

A year later, the major deportations began. A local Jewish theater, the Hollandse Schouwburg, became the assembly point from which Jews were shipped east to death. Some Dutch Christian families hid Jewish families, others abetted the German efforts to uncover them. Of the 80,000 Jews who lived in Amsterdam before World War II, about 5000 survived. The Jewish community today has mostly moved out into newer sections of the city. Post-war redevelopment projects demolished most of the buildings that were still standing, erasing almost every trace of the world that once thrived here. Yet some signs remain in the area near the Waterlooplein, the Visserplein and the Jodenbreestraat. There are some sparks of renewal which, if not recreating a vanished world, at least serve to preserve its memory.

In the center of the Visserplein stands the grand **Portuguese Synagogue**. It can be reached by tram 9, or bus 56. This synagogue and the complex of German synagogues

THE JEWISH QUARTER

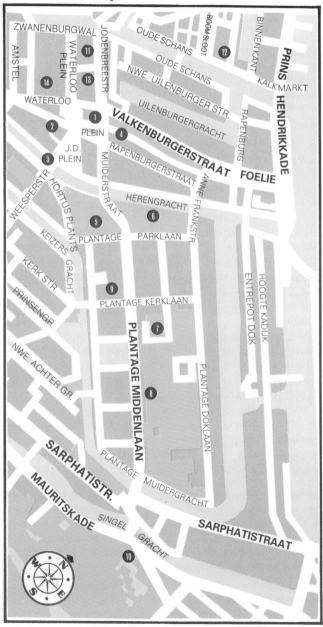

across the street, are among the few remnants of a bygone world. This was the center of the thriving Jewish community.

The Portuguese Synagogue was completed in 1675 in a period when such an overtly Jewish building could not be built elsewhere in Europe. 17th-century paintings show it standing proud and apart, surrounded by trees and bordering the canal and bridge that ran between it and the German synagogues. It is a huge, high, red-brick edifice, with a facade clearly stating its Jewish nature. It testifies to the wealth and the general status of at least some sectors of the Sephardic Jewish community, and to the tolerance of the city of Amsterdam.

Designed by a city architect, Elias Bouman, it was modeled along the lines of Solomon's Temple. Inside, the high barrel vaults give an impression of tremendous space, and a steady light flows through the many arched windows and illuminates the huge hall. The supporting columns and seats face the massive carved ark for the Torah scrolls. The brass chandeliers which hang from the vaulted roof date from the synagogue's earliest days. The synagogue was restored between 1953 and 1959.

The synagogue is one of Amsterdam's famous old buildings, and had already been declared a national monument before World War II, an injunction which the Nazis respected, surprisingly enough.

The synagogue today scrapes together enough people for prayers on the Sabbath. The synagogue is not always open when it is supposed to be, which is daily 10am-1pm except Saturdays and Jewish holidays. Sometimes it only appears closed. Ring the bell on the side, and if that doesn't work, try a few strong knocks on the door. Modest dress is required, as are head coverings for men. No photography is allowed inside.

An annex building houses the **Ets Haim Library** ('Tree of Life' in Hebrew). The library dates from 1616 and is a storehouse of Jewish history. Its famous and priceless collection of books, engravings and manuscripts was shipped to Germany during the war, but amazingly it was largely recovered. The library is still an active study center.

Four Ashkenazi synagogues are just across from the Portugese synagogue. Together, these buildings formed the social and spiritual center of the Jewish community. The four synagogues were built between 1670-1752, to accommodate the expanding Ashkenazi population, which had outgrown its early facilities and surpassed the Sephardic community in size. These synagogues, unlike the Portuguese synagogue, were plundered and vandalized during World War II.

In 1987, the **Jewish Historical Museum** was moved from its cramped quarters in the Waag at the Nieuwmarkt to these synagogues, which have been renovated and joined into one complex.

The displays depict Jewish tenets, festivals and ceremonies, Jewish history, the Holocaust, Zionism and the role of Israel, as well as the history of the Amsterdam Jewish community. A display of Dutch Jewish art includes some superb works. The works of Charlotte Salomon are displayed here. In the Grote Shule, the first and largest of the synagogues, there is an extremely beautiful marble ark. (2-4 Jonas Daniel Meijerplein. Open daily 11am-5pm. Museumcard valid. Tel. 26 99 45.) The displays on the diamond industry illustrate early polishing and cutting methods as well as the role of the diamond trade in the development of local Jewish life. It is an excellent exhibition, which succeeds in capturing the spirit of the times.

The small bookstore offers a nice selection of books on Jewish subjects, and the kosher coffee shop serves light meals. The ginger pastries are an Amsterdam Jewish speciality.

In the Meijerplein stands the sculpture, the **Dockworker**, by Mari Andriessen, with the Portuguese Synagogue in the background. The stocky, powerful figure conveys the determination with which Amsterdam's dockworkers faced the Nazis in a protest strike against the first deportations of Jews. The statue is not only a monument to those workers who attempted to stop the murder machine, but also serves as a warning against oppression. Every February 25th, a ceremony is held at the sculpture to commemorate the resistance against the Nazis.

The **Waterlooplein flea market** is temporarily to be found along the demolished section of the Rapenburgerstraat opposite the Visserplein. The market has lost its original charm and bustle

— and its bargains. It may regain some of its original flavor when it returns to its original location on the Waterlooplein. Today one can find reject jeans and denim jackets, cheap stereo equipment and cassettes, cheap hash pipes imported from India, and scented candles, usually at less than the retail price. Anything antique, or resembling an antique, is expensive, and the sellers can be aggressive and downright insulting. There is still a thriving business in cheap used bicycles, most of them stolen.

The Muiderstraat leads from the Visserplein towards a green area which includes Wertheim Park and the city's Botanical Gardens. The whole area, known as the **Plantage**, was once green and country-like and was intended to remain a park, but it was slowly built up. It became a quiet middle-class extension of the old Jewish quarter.

The **Botanical Gardens**, under the auspices of the Amsterdam University, is a fine garden with over 2000 species of trees, exotic flowers, herbs, etc. There are several tropical greenhouses with well-laid out paths. The small cafe is a verdant spot for a cup of coffee. Nominal admission.

Wertheim Park, is named after a well-known banker and philanthropist, who alloted an hour each day to making himself available to anyone who required his financial assistance.

Further along is the **Artis**, a pretty and interesting zoo. It can be reached by tram 9 or bus 56. (Open 1 May-30 Sept. daily 9am-6pm, 1 Oct.-30 April daily 9am-4:30pm. The entrance is off Plantage Kerklaan, perpendicular to the Plantage Middenlaan.) The zoo was founded by a group called Natura Artis Magistra, meaning 'nature is the instructor of art'. It was intended to give the urban community a better understanding of the world of nature. From 1838 until 1937 it was only open to members, but for over fifty years it has been open to the public. Most of the animals live in enclosures which resemble, as much as possible, their natural habitats. There is also a fine selection of tropical birds and a children's farm where a variety of domestic and barnyard animals can be played with and tended.

The building adjacent to the zoo held the city register of Amsterdam during World War II, with records of the city's Jews. In March 1943, a resistance group attacked the building. The records were set aflame, but the tightly packed registration cards did not ignite. The group was betrayed, and twelve members were arrested and executed.

The **Zoological Museum** is fair and not likely to be a major

Bicycles, Bicycles and more Bicycles

stop for the Amsterdam visitor, unless one happens to be in the neighborhood. The museum can be entered from the zoo, or from Plantage Middenlaan, with a separate entrance fee for those entering from the street without going to the zoo.

On the Plantage Middenlaan near Plantage Kerklaan stands the shell of the **Hollandse Schouwburg**, a theater which featured mainly Jewish artists performing for largely Jewish audiences. The theater became the major assembly point for the deportation of Jews to the death camps during the war. Post-war plans to use it as a cinema sparked strong and emotional opposition, and it now stands as a stark monument to those who died. An obelisk rises from a Star of David, and an eternal flame burns behind a glass window. The earth and plants in this chamber come from Israel. The three tombstones symbolize a father, mother and child. Nearby is a Dutch and Hebrew inscription, which translates as *"My soul cries with grief/Raise me up to Your world"*.

The **Tropenmuseum** (Tropical Museum) is not part of the Jewish quarter, but it is easily accessible from here along the Plantage

Middenlaan. Continue straight along Plantage Mi[...]
cross the Plantage Muidergracht and the Singe[...]acht. Bear
right until you reach Linnaeusstraat, and you'll see the museum.
Tram 9 connects the Waterlooplein with the Tropenmuseum.
Trams 3, 6 and 10 also run to or near the museum, as does bus
22.

The building itself is impressive, with several floors of galleries
surrounding a wide, open atrium through which light pours. The
Tropenmuseum is an exciting, colorful and innovative museum.
Established in the last century as a showcase for artifacts
from the Dutch Colonies, the museum today views the myriad
cultures and peoples within the Third World.

One walks through the separate exhibits which cover Africa,
Latin America, the Middle East, and South and Southeast Asia. In
each, indigenous environments are colorfully and meticulously
recreated. In the Beduin encampment you can almost smell
the camels, and in the Arab market you'll be tempted to
start bargaining. You walk through a Calcutta shantytown of
cardboard and corrugated iron, and a Caribbean farmhouse of
scavenged boards.

Some exhibits unite diverse regions through a central theme on
a cultural motif, such as the role of music or rituals surrounding
death. Others focus on man's relationships to a particular kind of
environment. There is, for example, a fascinating and disturbing
display on the fragile ecology of rain forests, and their steady
denuding, from Pakistan to the Amazon.

With lots of direct stimulus and hands-on learning, it's an ideal
for children as well, and there is a special **Children's Museum**,
which adults can enter only if accompanied by a minor! The
Children's Museum caters especially to children in the age
group of 6-12. Every 2 to 3 years the Children's Museum features
a new exhibition such as the recent one on China, Hong Kong
and the Chinese in the Netherlands.

The museum has an interesting library featuring material related
to the museum's fields of interest, and next door is a large
cafeteria. A bookstore sells guides to the museum.

Every season, five special days are organized during which
visitors are offered extensive information on traveling through a
particular country or region in the Third World.

Located at 2 Linnaeusstraat. Open Mon.-Fri., 10am-5pm. Sat.,
Sun. and holidays, noon-5pm. The Children's Museum is open
on Sunday, holidays and summer vacations, noon-4pm. On

Saturdays, special programs are organized, and entry is by reservation. Admission 5 fl. Discounts to youth and seniors. Museumcard valid. Tel. 56 88 200. Children's Museum, Tel. 56 88 300.

The **Soeterijn**, the theater of the Royal Tropical Institute, provides multi-media coverage of themes concerning relations between non-western and western countries. There is an ongoing schedule of theater, films, music, dance, lectures, and discussions.

Back by the Visserplein, walk east down the Jodenbreestraat to the Uilenburg, an area of early wharves and shipyards, which was later settled by the Jews. The massive brick building at the edge of the Uilenburgergracht is the shell of the gigantic Boaz Diamond Works, at one time the biggest in the city.

Just down from the Boaz works is an old synagogue which functioned as both a social and a religious center until 1943. Plundered during the war but later restored by the city council, the building is now a restoration studio, and has an exhibition on restoration crafts which is open to the public. Today the area which was once interspersed with factories and slums is quiet and boarded up — a pretty but slightly dubious area to stroll through.

At the end of the Jodenbreestraat, by the Oude Schans, is a 1606 brick building, three stories high, which, from 1639-1659, was the home of Rembrandt.

Rembrandthuis was part of a respectable, upper-middle class neighborhood when it was purchased by the newly married Rembrandt. (4-6 Jodenbreestraat. Open Mon.-Sat. 10am-5pm, Sun. and public holidays 1-5pm. Museumcard valid. Tel. 24 94 86.) Gradually the house became part of the rapidly filling Jewish quarter. It was among these Jews from all over the world that Rembrandt found the models for his biblical scenes.

A visit to the house can only give one an idea of what it must have been like when Rembrandt lived here, when the ground floor alone was lined with more than a hundred paintings that he bought.

This house witnessed success but also great pain and tragedy. Three of the four children born to Rembrandt and his wife Saskia died in this house. Saskia herself died, at age 32.

When Rembrandt's fortunes fell, to the point of bankruptcy, he was forced to leave his home of some twenty years, for the poor and crowded working-class district of the Jordaan.

It is Rembrandt's etchings, rather than his paintings, which form the bulk of the collection here. These form a major part of Rembrandt's vast production, and his vision as an artist emerges in these works. The exhibits explain the complex process of creating an etching. This medium made his work far more accessible than his paintings. Rembrandt's etchings were in high demand, and, through prints in books, reached a wide audience.

The etching process is more flexible than engraving, and Rembrandt fully exploited its great potential. His etchings ranged from landscape to daily life to scriptural subjects. He created effects of wind blowing through the trees, of tumbling clouds, of luminous sunbeams splitting the darkness, and in some of his etchings, parts of the picture are almost abstract patterns of light and dark, with only the subject itself clearly drawn.

In the basement an informative slideshow is presented alternately in English and Dutch. At the counter bookstore English pamphlets are available, as are reproductions of Rembrandt prints, some for as little as 2 fl. Guided tours are available on request.

The view from Rembrandt's house could have come right from one of his etchings of Amsterdam. From this point, the Sint Antoniesluis, one gazes over the wide Oude Schans as it flows toward the harbor. Across the canal, the Montelbaanstoren breaks the low horizon. With one of the most photographed views in the city, the small square is a picturesque spot to eat a picnic lunch. A natural food store just a block up from the Rembrandthuis has delicious take-aways. Next to the Rembrandthuis and across the canal are several cafes with good views of the Oude Schans.

One street to the west of the Jodenbreestraat is the border of the old Waterlooplein, (a cross street also bears the name Waterlooplein, so don't get confused). The two streets bordered what was once the old flea market of Amsterdam, and glass and concrete buildings now stand in place of the lively stalls.

This street, like the adjacent Jodenbreestraat, was the heart of the earliest Jewish quarter dating back to the 17th century. Along the Waterlooplein itself, few signs remain of the neighborhood that once thrived here. In the earliest synagogue in Amsterdam, which once stood on this street, the young Jewish philosopher Spinoza was excommunicated from the Jewish community. It is thought that he was born in 1632, in one of the houses which once stood near the Mozes-en-Aaronkerk, which is located at

A subtle blend of old and new styles

the corner of the Waterlooplein and the Visserplein.

The **Mozes-en-Aaronkerk** (Moses and Aaron Church) started as a clandestine Catholic church. Father Boelenzs bought two houses from a Jewish merchant in the Jewish Quarter and converted them into a chapel in 1649. This unexpected patchwork of religious minorities is partly what comprised the unique social and religious fabric of Amsterdam. It was only in 1841 that the Church was expanded and rebuilt in a neoclassic design. Some of the stones and gablestones of the original 17th century secret chapel were reused in the present building. The church today has become a sort of alternative social and activity center for youths, and a focal point for foreigners seeking help.

The new ultra-modern entertainment center, **Het Muziektheater**, opened in 1986. The complex includes the new Stadhuis (Town Hall), a cafe, restaurant, shops, etc. The new theater is home to the Dutch Opera, the National Ballet and the Dutch Dance Company. Internationally known companies also perform here, and there are usually special performances for the annual Holland Festival in June (Tel. 55 18 911).

Ticket office opens Mon.-Sat. at 10am, Sun. at 12am. Tickets are also available from the VVV and the AUB on the Leidseplein. The Waterlooplein Metro station is near the theater. There is a car-park under the theater. Box office Tel. 25 54 55.

Excursions

The Netherlands is a small country, with an excellent public transportation system. Many of the main population centers and tourist sights are clustered along the coast, between Amsterdam in the north and Rotterdam in the south. Rotterdam, The Hague, Delft, Leiden, Haarlem, and the tulip fields are all within easy reach. Along the winding shore of the Zuider Zee, in the peninsula north of Amsterdam, and on the Texel island there are tiny villages, some with their own special charm. They are accessible by bicycle, bus or car. Some of these, such as Marken and Volendam, have become major tourist attractions. North of the Zuider Zee (IJsselmeer) lies Friesland, a separate world clinging to its own language. Most excursions from Amsterdam can easily be done within a day, so it's possible to return to Amsterdam to sleep. There is, of course, accommodation in most villages and towns, and local offices of the VVV can provide information on tour routes, sights and hotels.

There are several bus companies which run organized tours from Amsterdam. Most of these leave from the vicinity of the Dam Square or the Stationsplein. Depending on the length and route of the tour, these excursions can cost between 25 and 50 fl.

They tend to be typical commercial tours, which visit spots crowded with busloads of tourists from other companies, milling around the same centers, browsing through the same tourist-oriented shops. Certain spots are standard tourist stops: the weekly Alkmaar cheese market, the fishing villages of Marken and Volendam, a wooden shoe workshop, the porcelain works at Delft. The guiding is multi-lingual and varies in quality, but in general there is an emphasis on going to places where passengers can buy, whether it be cheese, wooden clogs or chinaware. In Rotterdam and The Hague, the tour basically consists of a drive and perhaps a walk through certain areas, with explanations from the guide. On such tours, one only sees the fine-art museums of The Hague from the outside.

Although superficial, these tours are recommended for those with limited time, or who simply do not feel like hassling with train schedules, etc. They provide a wide and informative overview, and they also allow passengers to relax and enjoy the green and lush Dutch countryside. A good guide can, of course, increase one's understanding of the fascinating and complex system of dikes, channels and polders (land reclaimed from the sea) which comprises western Holland.

Nearby Outings

One simple excursion is to the **Amsterdamse Bos**, within the city limits but far from the center of the city. This huge hand-planted forest, created as part of the public work program in the 1930s, is a major recreational center for Amsterdammers, and is one of those wonderful spots in the middle of a city where one can escape the bustle and noise. The trees which make up acres of deciduous woodland were imported from the northeastern United States and eastern Canada. It's a great place for boating, cycling, hiking, and jogging. Bicycle rental is available in the park or one can come by bike from Amsterdam. It's a scenic and easy ride. The countryside is green, lush, picturesque and, perhaps most important, flat. You can ride along easily for hours and just let the farms and green fields glide gently by. The **Bosmuseum** presents exhibits on the natural history of the forest and its life systems. It is also an information center for the park. (Open 10am-5pm daily. Tel. 43 14 14. It can be reached by bus 70.)

South of the Bos, and outside the city limits, is the famous and huge **Aalsmeer Flower Auction**. (World Flower Center V.B.A. Nominal admission. Opening hours vary. Can be reached by bus C71.) This is the world's largest flower auction, and in fact, the largest commercial building in the world. It is a fascinating place to visit, giving a behind-the-scenes glimpse of Holland's huge flower business, which comprises a cooperative of over 4,000 plant and flower growers. Every night and early morning cases and truckloads of flowers pour into the center, up and down halls so long that trucks and bikes are used to get from one end to another. The visitor follows a catwalk suspended above the warehouse floor, gazing down at long lines of carts spilling over with roses, carnations, lilacs and freesias. The auction rooms use clocks hooked up to a computer system and the auctions seem to run at breakneck speed. The whole process of arrival, display, auctioning, payment, packaging and transferral to large aircraft containers is so efficient that freshly picked flowers brought to auction before dawn can be standing in a corner flower stall in New York that same night. It is best to visit in the early morning. Every year on the first Saturday of September the *Bloemencorso* (flower festival) takes place, which includes a flower parade from Aalsmeer to Amsterdam and back.

South of Amsterdam

Haarlem

Haarlem is only a twenty-minute train ride west of Amsterdam, yet it has its own special atmosphere. In spite of having over 150,000 residents, the old, medieval center retains a calm, village-like quality. Built within a system of protective canals, like Amsterdam, Haarlem too prospered in the 17th century. It also became a center for art, developing its own distinctive school.

Haarlem is the capital of the province of North Holland. From here it is easy to travel to the northern islands. The beach resort of **Zandvoort**, and a national park of dunes are within easy reach, as are the extensive tulip fields to the south.

Trains run at frequent intervals to Haarlem from Amsterdam. The VVV is located to the right of the main exit toward the center of town. This office is particularly well stocked, with a lot of information and maps. Public transportation runs from the station to the old center of Haarlem, where most of the main sights are found. Since this whole old section is concentrated into about one square kilometer, it is preferable to walk.

The **Grote Markt** (Great Market) marks the center of the medieval city, and it is stunning. Some of the finest examples of northern Renaissance architecture are found here. Several old streets which converge at the center have been turned into shopping areas, with many restaurants and cafes in the old gabled houses. Perhaps the most striking building on the square is the **Vleeshal** (Meat Hall), with its burnished step-gabled facade, interlaced with contrasting whitish stonework. Vleeshal and the adjacent **Vishal** (Fish Hall) are now annexes of the Frans Hals Museum, with free exhibits of modern art.

Near the edge of the Grote Markt looms the **Church of St. Bavo.** (Open Mon.-Sat., May-Aug. 10am-4pm, Sept.-April 10am-3:30pm.) Parts of this huge edifice date back to the 14th and 15th centuries, though most of it was constructed later. The church is breathtaking both in size and in detail. There are numerous chapels around the main hall. On the left wall beside the Font Chapel, note the cannonball, probably lodged there during the siege of Haarlem in 1572-73. The world-famous Christiaan Mueller organ contains 5,000 pipes and was played by an 11-year old Mozart, as well as by Handel and Albert Schweitzer. The organ is still played in concerts. Buried beneath the church's huge flagstones are the artist Frans Hals and a group of Haarlem's cobblers.

Aalsmeer Flower Auction - the largest in the world

Facing the church from across the square is the **Stadhuis** (Town Hall), where one can see the different structures which were added over the centuries starting from the 14th-century. (Open weekdays 9am-5pm.)

Beyond the Grote Markt, bordering a canal, is the **Frans Hals Museum**, housed in one of the many *hofjes* (almshouses) that once graced Haarlem. (62 Groot Heiligland. Open daily 11am-5pm, Sun. and holidays 1-5pm. Entrance 4 fl, discounts for children and seniors over 65. Tel. 023-31 91 80.) Buses 1, 2, 3, 4, 6, 8, 71 and 72 reach the museum.

The collection of paintings is remarkable. Frans Hals was breaking new artistic ground at the same time that his contemporary Rembrandt was making artistic breakthroughs. This museum is undoubtedly the highlight of a visit to Haarlem. The main Haarlem masters are represented here, though there are also exhibits of modern art which are at least as impressive as those found in Amsterdam's Stedelijk Museum.

Hals supposedly lived out his life in the very *hofje* that houses his masterpieces. He lived a wild, bohemian life, and left behind a spate of illegitimate children and debts. One of his most famous group portraits, the *Civic Guard of St. Adrian in Haarlem*, painted in 1633, hangs in the museum. What is most amazing in this portrait, beyond the lively contrast of color in the officers' silk sashes, is the individuality of character and expression.

The **Teylers Museum** is Holland's oldest museum, with sections dating from the late 18th century. (16 Spaarne. Open Tues.-Sat. 10am-5pm, Sun. 1-5pm. From Oct. to Feb., museum closes at 4pm. Admission 3l, discounts for children and seniors. Museumcard valid. Tel. 023-31 68 51.) The museum depicts an age when scientific exploration was revealing much about the world, and these discoveries were understood as having both moral and artistic import. The lines between art, science and philosophy were thin. Scientific thinkers were just beginning to be aware of the vastness of the natural world, and Europe was filled with amateur collectors attempting to categorize and detail this newly discovered world.

The collections in the Teylers Museum are diverse and huge, consisting of gems, fossils, early prints, telescopes and models of the solar system, mechanical models and gadgets, electric generators and old Leyden jars. The halls and exhibit cabinets are ornate and polished. In addition, there is also a collection of drawings by Italian masters such as Michaelangelo and Raphael.

On the first Sunday of each month, at 3pm, a concert of voice and organ is given.

Tulip Fields — South of Haarlem
South of Haarlem runs the long strip of tulip country. During the springtime the rows of flowers are like a rainbows with long contrasting bands running brightly along, seemingly forever. The countryside bursts with color and swarms with tourists. Haarlem makes a convenient base for a bicycle ride through the tulip country, as does the town of **Lisse**. In the springtime be sure not to miss the verdant **Keukenhof** flower garden there. You may never want to leave this bubble of paradise with its forests and lawns. For two months, from the end of March, a steady succession of flowers open: crocuses and hyacinths, narcissi and, of course, tulips.

The tulip, by the way, is not indigenous to the Netherlands. Brought from Turkey in the 16th century, they found an ideal habitat in the sandy soil along the dunes of the North Sea coast.

The dunes are easily accessible from Lisse by bicycle, car or public transportation. The resort towns are nothing special, but the dunes around Noordwijkaan Zee offer an open expanse for some barefoot wandering.

The Lisse VVV office is located at 53a Grachtweg, Tel. 025-21 14 562.

Leiden

On a branch of the Rhine as it approaches the sea between Haarlem and The Hague is Leiden. As in Haarlem, the city's well-preserved medieval center lends it the atmosphere of a small, quiet town, a feeling enhanced by the presence of Holland's oldest university. There is a subdued, academic atmosphere in the old streets and narrow alleys. The buildings of the university have been finely preserved. There is a concentration of museums here, some more specialized than others but most are of a very high caliber. It is unlikely that a visitor would want to visit them all, however.

Leiden is easily reachable by train from Haarlem or Amsterdam. The VVV can provide a complete list of a wide range of local accommodation and restaurants. (210 Stationsplein. Open April-August, Mon.-Sat., 9am-6pm. Sept.-March, Mon.-Fri., 9am-5:30pm, Sat. 10am-4pm. Tel. 071-14 68 46.) Near the station are facilities for renting bicycles. Various companies offer boat rides through the old town's moats and canals and across the major lakes.

Although the town existed as early as in the 12th century, most buildings do not go back beyond the 14th century. It was in 1575 that the town was awarded with a university for its long and valiant defense against a Spanish siege. The **Academie**, the main building of the university, stands gracefully next to the pretty **Rapenburg Canal**. The Rapenburg, along with the Breestraat and Steenchur, are the outer boundaries of medieval Leiden. Across the Rapenburg from the Academie stands the **Rijksmuseum van Oudheden** (National Antiquities Museum). (28 Rapenburg. Open Tues.-Sat. 10am-5pm. Sun. and public holidays 1-5pm. Museumcard valid.) This is the main museum in the city, and the major archeological museum in the country. The collection of Egyptian wall reliefs, mummies, sarcophagi and so forth is tremendous and fascinating.

Look out for the huge, imposing **Sint Pieterskerk** in the central square. Parts of it date back to the 14th century. Buried here is John Robinson, spiritual father of the pilgrims who made their way on the *Mayflower* to the freedom of America. Robinson lived in a house on the site of the **Jan Pesijn Hofje**, adjacent to the church and one of many *hofjes* in the old town. Adhering to the principles of freedom of worship, Robinson met hostility both in his native England and in relatively tolerant Holland. The first group of his disciples left in 1620, but their mentor died before setting sail. Records and exhibits dealing with the man and the Pilgrim Fathers can be seen in the **Pilgrim Fathers Documents Center**. (45 Vliet. Open Mon.-Fri. 9:30am-4:30pm. Tel. 071-13 44 21.)

The municipal museum is in the old **Lakenhal**, which once served as the guild hall of the town's clothmakers. (28-32 Oude Singel. Open Tues.-Sat. 10am-5pm., Sun. 1-5pm. Nominal entrance fee. Tel. 071-25 46 20.) It contains a gallery devoted to the town's well-known painters, including a separate room which focuses on Rembrandt. Rembrandt left Leiden at a young age to be apprenticed as an artist in Amsterdam. He returned here to set up his own studio, and soon gained a reputation as an extremely promising and talented young painter. His ambition, however, took him once again to Amsterdam. The well-preserved second floor has some interesting exhibits on old weaving techniques.

The **Royal Army and Weapon Museum** covers, in a surprisingly interesting manner, the gruesome subject of wars — from the Dutch wars during the Spanish invasion to modern colonial incursions. (7 Pesthuislaan. Open Mon.-Fri. 9:30am-5pm. Nominal admission.)

The **Rijksmuseum Voor Volkenkunde** (National Museum of Ethnology), focuses largely on areas of former Dutch colonization, an unexpectedly large area. (1 Steenstraat. Open Tues.-Sat. 10am-5pm, Sun. and public holidays 1-5pm. Admission. Tel. 071-13 26 41.)

The main shopping area, from the Breestraat to the Haarlemmerstraat, contains many small cafes and restaurants, with several that are reasonably priced.

The Hague

Although Amsterdam is the nation's capital, The Hague, or Den Haag, is the seat of government and diplomatic center, as well as the home of the queen. With a slightly smaller population than Amsterdam and Rotterdam, it has a special dignified charm.

There are, of course, exciting cultural events in The Hague, but most visitors confine themselves to a day visit to see the best-known buildings and museums. There are a large number of museums, the most famous being the Mauritshuis. The North Sea Jazz Festival is a major event held here every June.

In keeping with its position as the residency of royalty and diplomats, The Hague tends to be more expensive than the other major cities. Less expensive accommodation and place to eat can be found in the adjacent Scheveningen.

The main VVV office is located next to the Centraal Station, in the Babylon Shopping Center at 30 Koningin Julianaplein. However, trains arriving from Amsterdam do not stop at this station but rather at the Hollands Spoor Station. From there, tram 12 goes to the VVV, and trams 5, 8 and 9 go to the city center. A branch of the tourist office is found at the Scheveningen resort at 2 Zwolsstraat (next to the *Europa Crest Hotel*). There is one general number for tourist information, Tel. 070-54 62 00. For public transportation information and train details, Tel. 070-82 41 41.

The center of The Hague is indisputably the **Binnenhof**, or inner court. Palaces, portals, spires and banners decorate this 13th-century compound. One can almost hear the hoofs of the knights' horses echoing heavily on the stones. Here, every September, the reigning monarch arrives by golden coach to open the session of parliament. The **Ridderzaal** (Knights' Hall), has been renovated and used for many different purposes over the years, so that only fragments of its 13th-century structure remain. Still, it is quite impressive outside and in, and is a fine example of northern Gothic architecture. The guided tour through the hall begins with an audiovisual presentation and enters the Hall of the Knights and the First and/or Second Chambers of the States General. (Open Mon.-Sat. 10am-4pm. Closed Sun. and public holidays. Admission depends on the length of the tour, from 1.50-4.50 fl. Reservations for tours should be made by phone. The last tour starts at 3:55pm. Tel. 070-64 61 44.)

Also in the Binnenhof courtyard is the **Mauritshuis**, known throughout Europe as one of the best of the small art museums. (Open Tues.-Sat. 10am-5pm. Sun. and holidays 11am-5pm. Before mid-May, admission is 3.50 fl. Through summer, admission 5 fl. Discounts for children and seniors. Museumcard valid. Tel. 070-46 92 44.) The building, recently renovated, was, in the 17th century, the residence of the Dutch governor for the colony in Brazil. Hanging here is a superb, selective collection of paintings from the Dutch Golden Age, including one of Rembrandt's early masterpieces, *Dr. Tulp's Anatomy Lesson*. Although not his most famous, his *Portrait of Homer* is particularly striking in its uncanny portrayal of those sightless eyes.

Hanging here, too, and mysterious in its own way, is Vermeer's glowing and peaceful *View of Delft*. (The guided tours take

The Hague - Binnenhof

Madurodam

you past the house that he painted.) He managed to approach the objects and furnishings of everyday life with something approaching reverence. Also included are paintings by Jan Steen, Frans Hals, and masters from the Flemish School such as Rubens, Van Dyck, and others.

Walk all the way through the Binnenhof, and be sure to look at the reflections of the huge medieval structures in the waters of the Hof Vijver Lake.

North of the Binnenhof stands the **Paleis Noordeinde**, the home of the Dutch royal family. The Queen has another home just outside of town. The palace can only be seen from the outside.

Just beyond it, a little further north, is a palace of a different kind. The **Vredespaleis** (Peace Palace) is the home of the International Court of Justice. Built in 1913 through the generosity of Scottish-American steel tycoon Andrew Carnegie, the building is magnificent, if somewhat eerie. (Open Mon.-Fri. 10am-noon, 2-4pm. Guided tours at 10 and 11am, noon, 2pm and 3pm. From 11 June-Sept. also at 4pm. Sat. and Sun. for groups only, upon request. Admission 3 fl. Discounts for children. Tel. 070-46 96 80.)

The turrets and towers, the multiple arches of the facade, are hard to appreciate fully when the history of the last 70 years is contrasted with the ideals that this building symbolized. For even as the nations of Europe and the world were furnishing the palace, they were involved in the arms build-up which preceded War I.

The **Haagse Gemeentemuseum** (Municipal Museum) contains a fine collection of modern art, including the largest collection in the world of works by the Dutch pioneer of abstract and plastic art, Piet Mondriaan. There are also works by Henry Moore, Picasso and Monet, and a remarkable collection of musical instruments from both the East and West. (Open Tues.-Fri. 10am-5pm. Sun. and holidays, noon-5pm. Admission 2 fl. Discounts to children and seniors. Museumcard valid. Tel. 070-51 41 81.)

Also well worth a visit is the 19th-century panoramic reproduction of what was once the tiny fishing village of Scheveningen. (65b Zeestraat. Open Mon.-Sat. 10am-5pm. Sun. and holidays noon-5pm. Admission 3 fl. Discount for children. Tel. 070-64 25 63.) The huge circular canvas was painted by the famous marine painter H.W. Mesdag, assisted by his wife and other painters. Once a common form of optical illusion, it creates a surprising sense of depth and reality.

The real beach at **Scheveningen** is nowhere as quaint as the painted version. It is a recently redone resort that is both fancy and sleazy. Dominated by the huge Kurhaus Casino built in 1885, it is a Dutch Atlantic City, and can easily be left out of your intinerary.

Madurodam

Madurodam, just outside The Hague, is the famous scale-model of Dutch towns and landmarks, very touristy, but delightful as well. If you missed one of the famous Dutch monuments you can see it here! Whole cities and quaint village squares are superbly reproduced with incredible detail, down to the flowers and pigeons perched on the roof tops — children will love it. (175 Haringkade. 26 March-31 May, 9am-10pm. June-Aug., 9am-10:30pm. Sept., 9am-9pm. 1-25 Oct., 9am-6pm. Admission 8 fl. Discounts to children. Special night shows in late spring and summer are a little more expensive. Tel. 070-55 39 00.)

Delft

Delft, once a small village, is now almost an extension of The Hague. Its old town center is immensely popular with tourists, largely due to the world-renowned reputation of Delftware, the blue and white hand-painted ceramics which were inspired by the styles from the Far East. Chinese techniques were adapted to a whole range of local and domestic Dutch imagery, and the blue and white porcelain images on tables, mantlepieces and mosaics are as automatically linked to Holland as are windmills and wooden clogs. Through the centuries, the local craftsmen have added to their palettes, and the multicolored pieces stand out after one has seen too much blue and white.

When the Delft industry was at its peak, 30 ceramic studios and workshops produced a vast array of objects, all with the blue and white design, and ranging from serving plates to delicate musical instruments. After the 18th century, however, the market began to shrink. Today there are only two studios producing original Delftware, of which only one is open to the public: *De Porceleyen Fles*, at 196 Rotterdamseweg. There are tours throughout the day, and visitors are welcomed to the showrooms. This is a regular stop on the organized tours from Amsterdam, and, of course, buying is greatly encouraged. The commercial aspect aside, however, it is indeed interesting to watch the craftmen working on the various painstaking stages in the production of this china. Prices for the pieces sold in the showroom are not cheap, but in the stores one can sometimes find seconds or slightly faulty pieces which one can buy relatively inexpensively. Authentic Delftware is marked with a special seal, and anything lacking that seal is an imitation. Check carefully if you buy from a store, as imitations abound.

Delft was the town in which the Dutch master painter Jan Vermeer (1632-1675) was born and lived. Almost all his works reflect simple, domestic Delft interiors and exteriors; the Delft he knew is even more elusive than the Amsterdam of his contemporary, Rembrandt. True, the tour buses stop at the gate which they claim appears in his famous painting *The Little Street* (which hangs in the Rijksmuseum in Amsterdam), but the resemblance is rather vague.

Vermeer painted simple people in the kitchens, courtyards and streets of Delft, but he invested these simple scenes with a timeless and monumental quality, and it is his superb perception and accurate portrayal of light, subtle tonal differences, and perspective which make him the outstanding master of Dutch naturalism. These sensitive and closely studied works of Vermeer inspired the Realists in the 19th century, who in turn inspired the Impressionists. Today, the town still has drawbridges and tree-lined canals, the typical central square, large churches, and narrow streets lined with medieval houses, but Delft has been overrun by tourists and tourist businesses.

The **Markt** is the center of the old town. Here the VVV office is to be found as well as many touristy cafes. At one end stands the **Stadhuis** (Town Hall), and at the other the **Nieuwe Kerk**. (Open Mon.-Sat. 9am-5pm. Nominal admission. Separate admission for tower.) Begun toward the end of the 14th century, it took a century to complete. William the Silent, founder of the Republic of the Netherlands in the late 16th century, is buried here. The steeple, 100 meters high, is open to the public and offers the best view you'll find of the quaint red-roofed town.

The 13th-century **Oude Kerk** on Hippolytusburt has an impressive vaulted interior and a leaning tower. (Open Mon.-Sat. noon-4pm. Nominal admission.) Do not miss the elaborately carved pulpit.

Opposite the church stands the **Prinsenhof**. (Open Mon.-Sat. 10am-5pm, Sunday 1-5pm. Admission 2 fl.) It was originally a convent, but from 1572 it was used by William the Silent during the Dutch revolt against Spanish rule. It was here, too, that he was shot in 1584, by an assassin paid by King Philip II of Spain. The bullets that lodged in the woodwork can still be seen today. The Prinsenhof also contains municipal art exhibits and exhibits from the Dutch rebellion.

If you wish to see more Delftware, visit **Museum Huis Lambert van Meerten**. (Located at 119 Oude Delft. Open Mon.-Sat. 10am-5pm., Sun. 1-5pm. Nominal admission.) The collection of

Rotterdam

pottery and tiles is vast and includes a tremendous variety of styles and patterns.

Rotterdam

Rotterdam is the southernmost of Holland's major cities, and is very close in size to Amsterdam — but it is a world apart.

When the Nazis invaded the Netherlands in 1940 they made an example of Rotterdam by completely razing it to the ground in bombing raids. The massive devastation did indeed spur the surrender of the Dutch army. After the war Rotterdam rebuilt itself from the rubble and became the largest port in the world. The skyline is composed of sleek, modern concrete towers and cranes and masts jutting up from the port. Raw materials and industrial goods pour through the loading docks. Tens of thousands of ships dock at Rotterdam each year, from all around the world. Its streets are wide and lined with concrete blocks. The sense of beauty it strives for is not traditional, but rather modern or futuristic. The module apartment buildings which stretch across the major highway are somehow appropriate to Rotterdam.

Athough Rotterdam has much to admire, there is simply not that much to see. Some of the bus excursions from Amsterdam weave through Rotterdam, and for those who simply want an overall glimpse of the city, this may be sufficient.

The VVV office is at 19 Stadhuisplein (Open daily 9am-6pm and

Fri. until 9pm during the summer season. Closed on Sunday from Oct-March. Tel. 010-413 60 00.) There is another office at the Centraal Station, open throughout the year (Mon.-Sat. 9-noon Sun. 10-noon. Tel. 010-413 60 06).

The city has one sight which is definitely worth seeing. The **Boymans-van Beuningen Museum** houses some incredibly beautiful art collections. (18 Mathenesserlaan. Open Tues.-Sat. 10am-5pm, Sun. and holidays 11am-5pm. Tel. 010-436 05 00.) Flemish masters including Brueghel and Bosch can be seen, and there are canvases by Rembrandt and others from the Dutch Golden Age, as well as such surrealist moderns as Salvador Dali. This is a wonderful museum and should not be missed.

A few small and specialized museums are found in **Delftshaven**, a small and charming old district in the midst of modernity. It was from this harbor from which the Pilgrim Fathers set sail for America.

About 32 km (20 miles) outside Rotterdam (accessible by bus 8 or by organized bus tour) is the **Delta Expo** at Haringvlietdam. This 2 km barrier was built as part of the huge Delta Project started in the wake of the 1953 flooding disaster. The exhibits clearly explain how the system of sluices and dams controls the outflow of river water and the inflow of seawater into the estuary. Details and organized tours are available from the VVV.

North of Amsterdam — Waterland

On the peninsula to the north of Amsterdam, the suburbs thin out quickly into flat countryside, with small towns and villages. This region, known as Waterland, is popular for bicycle day trips. There are several alternative routes here, carrying you past numerous windmills and small villages, to the villages of Hoorn, Marken, Monnickendam and others. Trips begin with a ferry ride from the Centraal Station across the IJ. Then you work your way along the city streets until the countryside takes over. The VVV can give you a detailed brochure with a route to follow, and they might have some other bicycling suggestions to make as well.

Several towns have become major tourist attractions. Most of the commercial bus companies operate tours that visit some if not all of these towns. They can also be reached by public transportation or automobile.

Marken

Marken, northeast of Amsterdam, was once a Calvinist fishing village isolated on a tiny island. It was later linked to the mainland by a dike, which encouraged tourism to the village. The village is fairly typical of a pristine village, with its own sober costumes and style of architecture. The little fishing harbor is lined with tourist shops. Away from the harbor, however, between the little houses, is a separate world of lush greenery, grazing goats, small arched bridges over the canals and neat little houses with scrubbed and shining front steps.

Volendam

Adjacent Volendam is a Catholic fishing village, with a totally different character. Here the atmosphere is less austere, the costumes much more colorful (there always seems to be someone standing around just waiting to be photographed!), and the tourist activity is on at a greater tempo. In the summer this town can get so flooded with tourists that it is not much fun to visit. But again, by wandering through the back streets you can get a better feel of the old village atmosphere. The **eel auction** is the main attraction here. Although it is questionable how attractive huge barrels of squirming, slimy eels can be, the auction is at least authentic.

Edam

Nearby Edam, famous for its cheese, is surprisingly quiet compared to Volendam. Like most of the villages here it is extremely picturesque. There's an old cheese weigh-house, displaying a few old pieces of paraphernalia, but the simple charm of the tiny village is reason in itself to visit.

Alkmaar

The real cheese capital — and tourist capital — of this peninsula is Alkmaar. Every Friday morning the tourist buses pull in with hundreds of camera-snapping tourists. By 10am it's too crowded to see anything. What most tourists come to see is teams of men dressed in white running with funny steps as they carry platforms that look like little boats, on which are piled huge shining nuggets of cheese. The men represent the different cheese guilds, and they bring the cheese to buyers and tasters who drill into the cheese to extract samples. On quieter days, Alkmaar becomes another peaceful town, worth strolling around, with a quick look into the **Cheese Museum**. The museum and the VVV are located in the local Waag (Weigh-House), which dates back to the 15th century, and was originally a church.

Texel

North of Alkmaar, the road runs to **Den Helder** at the

Conquering the sea with dikes

northwestern tip of the peninsula, where the ferry can be caught for the island of Texel. Texel, a lush island of forests, farmland and dunes, is a popular escape spot for both the Dutch and foreigners. During the summer the line for the ferry can be long. The island, however, is large enough to explore without feeling the crowds. Bicycle is the best way to travel around, and they can be hired in the main town, **Den Burg**. The VVV is also found there, in the small square. (Open Mon.-Fri. 9am-6pm, Saturday 9am-5pm.) The VVV can provide a list of hotels, rooms for rent, and campgrounds on the island.

Enkhuizen

East of this end of the peninsula, the **Afsluitdijk** stretches 19 miles across what was once the Zuider Zee and what is now an enclosed lake, called the IJsselmeer. The lake is gradually being filled with polders. The huge project changed the nature of the body of water and the way of life of the fishing villages and small ports along the peninsula's eastern shore. **Enkhuizen** is such a town. It was at one time the first sanctuary for ships rounding the bend from the North Sea. It had a strong defense system, remains of which can still be seen. At Enkhuizen the past is recreated at the **Zuider Zee Museum**, which preserves the way of life of the little villages. The museum, a popular stop, is divided into two: the Buitenmuseum (outdoor) and the Binnenmuseum (indoor). In the Buitenmuseum

Alkmaar - 'the cheese capital'

Marken

there are some 130 original buildings from the various villages which are presented in an authentic village setting. (Open from April to Oct., 10am-5pm daily.) The Binnenmuseum displays crafts, costumes, fishing vessels, etc. (Open end of May-Aug., 10am-5pm daily.) Both are interesting and do a careful job of preserving something that can no longer exist. (18 Wierdijk. Tel. 02280-10122. Entrance fee 9l for both parts. Museumcard valid.)

The VVV is located at the Centraal Station, and can provide information on boat rides across the IJsselmeer.

"MUSTS"

There are many things to see and do in Amsterdam and one could easily spend several weeks touring the city. For those whose time is limited, however, there are certain sights which are 'musts' for any visitor to Amsterdam. Each sight mentioned here is explained in greater detail in the section dealing with that area.

Anne Frankhuis (Anne Frank House): The house where Anne Frank and her family hid from the Nazis during World War II, and where she wrote her famous diary. A very moving and poignant experience. 263 Prinsengracht. Open June-August, Mon.-Sat. 9am-7pm, Sun. 10am-5pm; Sept.-May, Mon.-Sat. 9am-5pm, Sun. 10am-5pm. Entry 5 fl. Museumcard not valid. Tel. 26 45 33 (see 'The Jordaan — Dancing in the Street').

Koninklijk Paleis (Royal Palace): In the spacious halls of the palace can be seen masterpieces of 17th-century Amsterdam artists. The unimposing facade belies the lavish and magnificent interior rooms. Dam Square. Open daily 12:30-4pm. Sept.-May guided tours every Wed. at 2pm. Entry 1.50 fl. Tel. 24 86 98, ext. 217 (see 'The Dam Square — The Heart of the City').

Red-light District: Around Oudezijds Voorburgwal. Prostitutes sit in shop-windows, a scene unique to Amsterdam. Most interesting to visit at night (see 'East of Dam — Divinely Decadent').

Rijksmuseum: One of the finest art museums in Europe, including unparalleled masterpieces by Dutch Masters such as Rembrandt's *Night Watch*. 42 Stadhouderskade. Open Tues.-Sat. 10am-5pm, Sun. and holidays 1-5pm. Museumcard valid. Tel. 73 21 21 (see 'The Museumplein — Art Lovers' Paradise').

National Vincent Van Gogh Museum: Houses a collection of over 200 paintings and 500 drawings by Van Gogh. The presentation roughly follows Van Gogh's artistic development. 7 Paulus Potterstraat. Open Tues.-Sat. 10am-5pm, Sun. and holidays 1-5pm. Museumcard valid. Tel. 16 48 81 (see 'The Museumplein — Art Lovers' Paradise').

Another 'must' during your stay in Amsterdam is to take a **canal cruise** on a boat or paddle bike. This highly touristy activity is a lot of fun, especially for children (see 'Getting to Know the City').

See the city by boat

Tulip fields

Highly Recommended:

Amsterdams Historisch Museum (Amsterdam Historical Museum): Housed in an old orphanage. The exhibits range from the usual collections of artifacts to more innovative displays. Very worthwhile for those who want to gain some sense and understanding of Amsterdam's rise to power. Open Tues.-Sat. 10am-5pm, Sun. and holidays 1-5pm. Museumcard valid. Tel. 25 58 22 (see 'The Kalverstraat — Culture and Elegance').

Jewish Historical Museum: Recently moved to a refurbished complex of four old synagogues in what was once the original Jewish Quarter of the city. Several Jewish themes run through the exhibits. There is a display of very fine paintings by well-known Jewish Dutch artists and scenes from the neighborhood in its heyday. 2-4 Jonas Daniel Meijerplein. Open daily 11am-5pm. Museumcard valid. Tel. 26 99 45 (see 'The Jewish Quarter — Glimpse of a Vanished World').

Leidseplein: If you have but one night in Amsterdam, be sure to spend some of it here. The crowds, cafes and street entertainment reflect the spirit of Amsterdam (see 'The Leidseplein — Let the Good Times Roll').

Rembrandthuis: The former home of the artist, it contains a fine collection of the master's etchings. 4-6 Jodenbreestraat. Open Mon.-Sat. 10am-5pm, Sun. and holidays 1-5pm. Museumcard valid. Tel. 24 94 86 (see 'The Jewish Quarter — Glimpse of a Vanished World').

Tropenmuseum (Tropical Museum): A lively, visually stimulating museum with walk-through exhibits of third-world cultures and environments. 2 Linnaeusstraat. Open Mon.-Fri. 10am-5pm, Sun. and holidays noon-4pm. Museumcard valid. Tel. 58 38 200 (see 'The Jewish Quarter — Glimpse of a Vanished World').

Willet Holthuysen Museum: A visit here will give you an idea of the splendor and luxury that lay behind the dignified facades of Amsterdam's canal houses. 605 Herengracht. Open Tues.-Sat. 10am-5pm, Sun. and holidays 1-5pm. Museumcard valid. Tel. 26 42 90 (see 'The Rembrandtsplein — Museums and Nightlife').

Making The Most Of Your Stay

Wining and Dining

Although a comparatively small city, Amsterdam is packed with restaurants serving a huge range of cuisine, including Indonesian, Japanese, Greek, Turkish, Israeli, Yugoslavian, Fillipino, Pakistani, Chinese, Hungarian, Vietnamese, Mexican, French, American, Surinamese, Moroccan, Italian and, of course, Dutch.

The old-fashioned **Dutch** restaurants seem to have been hidden beneath the city's culinary exotica, but they can still be found. Some establishments serving basic, hearty Dutch meals do not really advertise themselves as restaurants at all, but rather as petite-restaurants, or simply *eetcafes*: cosy Dutch cafes and bars that also serve food. Dutch hotpots (stews) consist of potatoes, vegetables, meat and crisp fried bacon. Pan-fried beefsteak is popular, as are poultry and fish dishes, accompanied by vegetables, piles of home-fried potatoes, and ever-present apple sauce. Thick pea soup — *erwtensoep* — sprinkled with bits of meat, is a local winter favorite and almost a meal in itself. An *eetcafe* meal will cost about 15 fl, and you may feel unable to get up from your chair afterwards.

Pancake houses are numerous and popular, especially on Sunday mornings. Dutch pancake houses are often full for lunch, and some offer 'dinner pancakes'. Dutch pancakes make a tasty and hearty meal, especially the wholewheat ones. They are folded and filled with a variety of sweet or savory fillings. Street stands also sell pancakes and *poffertjes* (small doughnuts sprinkled with sugar).

Amsterdam offers a feast for **seafood** lovers. Both freshwater and saltwater fish are plentiful, as are oysters, mussels and shrimps. Perhaps most marvelous is the fine seafood to be purchased right on the street, at stands that can be found everywhere. Here you can buy shrimp, mussels and herring, in small containers or in sandwiches. At the Albert Cuypmarkt, there are carts full of various kinds of seafood, and it is possible to buy freshly smoked eel, another local favorite.

The Dutch have practically made a national pastime of eating *patats* (fried potatoes) served plain or with various sauces. The windows of sandwich shops and some bakeries are lined with ready made sandwiches (*broodjes*) on long rolls. All sorts of things may be piled on together: meats, cheese, eggs. They make a good fast lunch, but are sometimes surprisingly expensive.

Alternatively you can find a nice assortment of vegetables and fruits in the small grocery stores. Specialty shops are the best places to buy breads and cheeses and other delicacies, and going from one small shop to another is part of the life in Amsterdam. The dairy products are generally great. In addition to a variety of cheeses (many of them are a variation of the widespread Gouda and Edam cheeses) the yogurts are thick, creamy and filling.

This richness is also typical of the ice cream, which is fresh, delicious and creamy. The Dutch variation of apple pie, *applegebakeen* is popular and found in many coffee shops, pastry shops, etc., often at a special price for a cup of coffee and piece of pie.

Indonesian food is very popular and widespread; evidence of the strong influence of the former Dutch colonies. Indonesian food has almost become synonymous with Dutch food, and the Indonesian *rijsttafel*, or rice table, might be considered the national dish.

A *rijsttafel* may include over thirty exotic sauces, rich relishes and spicy meat dishes, accompanied by a mountain of rice. Some of the usual *rijsttafel* delicacies are *oblo-oblo* (made of soy beans), *daging bronkos* (roast meat in coconut sauce), and various spiced fish pastes. There are also precisely blended and spiced concoctions of chicken, nuts and vegetables. The *sateh* (skewers of cubed meat marinated in a peanut sauce) is a standard dish not only of the *rijsttafel*, but with other Indonesian dishes as well, and is very popular. *Sateh* variations (including a vegetarian one) are served in other restaurants besides Indonesian. A *rijsttafel* for two can come to 40-50 fl.

There are **pizzerias** all around Amsterdam, and many are concentrated along the streets branching off the Leidseplein. Pizza is served in a pleasant restaurant setting, with a muted and tastefully decorated interior, white tablecloths and candles, or at outdoor tables. Only a few pizzerias sell pizza by the slice. The pizzas are very reasonably priced, with a basic pizza, usually large enough for two, starting at 8-10 fl. Two people can order a combination pizza, salads and a beverage for about 20 fl.

Amsterdam has a large number of young health-conscious people, so healthy and gourmet **vegetarian** food is easy to find. Most vegetarian restaurants close about 9pm. More and more restaurants are featuring salad bars, some allowing unlimited servings. Seafood plates are offered in almost every kind of restaurant, and are popular with those who do not eat meat. Many Chinese, Indian, Indonesian and other East Asian eateries offer vegetarian platters, though true vegetarians should ask about the sauces used. A good Indonesian restaurant will often prepare a vegetarian version of the *rijsttafel*, usually at a lower price than the regular one.

There was a time when Amsterdam was filled with **kosher** restaurants, cafes, markets, butchers and delicatessens. These, however, with every other trace of vibrant Jewish life, disappeared under the Nazi onslaught. The few kosher restaurants and markets which remain are scattered around the city, but are mostly in the south, where the post-war centers of Jewish community shifted. Several are within access of the city's center and major tourist sights.

Amsterdam and **beer** go back a long way together, to the days when the frothy brew was consumed as a way to avoid drinking contaminated water. Amsterdam became a major port and toll point for the transport of beer from the Germanic and Scandinavian lands. The transport of beer, in fact, was one of the earliest contributing factors to Amsterdam's prosperity. Beer is as popular now as it ever was. The predominant local brew is undoubtedly Heineken, seconded by Amstel. A number of smaller labels are available, as are a wide selection of international beers in some cafes. Bought in a market, beer is very cheap. A glass in a cafe costs about 1.50-2.50 fl. The local Dutch gin is called *genever*, and is served in small shot glasses and tossed down with one sip.

The *bruine kroegs*, or brown cafes, are the most typical and characteristic of Amsterdam watering holes, blending the local love for beer, friendly company and tobacco. Named for the layers of nicotine that have stained the walls over the years, these cafes can be found in most of the older parts of the city. They are often low, dark and narrow places, with burnished old fixtures and kegs and low, thick, brown beams adding to the effect. In the afternoons when people get off from work these brown cafes are packed, and the neighborhood locals usually have their favorites, but outsiders are welcome. Some of these places have unique histories, having been in business for perhaps several hundred years.

These are not, of course, the only cafes in town. There are many new, trendy places where the tobacco smoke has not yet seeped in so deeply. Amsterdam has more than its share of these cafes with a sparser sense of design, modern art, decorations in neon script, and blaring punk music.

Restaurants

There are hundreds of restaurants to choose from in Amsterdam. They are clustered around the major public squares and tourist centers, spread along the charming canals or tucked into unexpected corners.

Although meals can be found for 15 fl or less, a meal between 20-35 fl with a beverage is considered average. Service charges are not included in the price, unless specifically stated otherwise (which is rare).

About 40 restaurants in the city offer a 'Tourist Menu', which is a set meal of several courses at a fixed price. The participating restaurants display a sign with a fork-and-camera insignia. These meals usually cost between 16.50 fl and 17.50 fl. They are not necessarily the most exciting dishes, but those that are typical of the specific cuisine of the restaurant and not too complicated to prepare. It is sometimes a good deal, but not always.

Dutch

Die Port van Cleve: 178-180 Nieuwezijd Voorburgwal. Tel. 24 48 60. Dating back more than 100 years, the walls and ceiling are pannelled in deeply-hued oak with beautiful carved edging. Above the wall panels, around the entire room, is an allegorical mural of Amsterdam, on blue Delft tiles. The restaurant is well-known for its steaks, in addition to thick pea soup. In winter old Dutch recipes are served: heavy dishes such as red cabbage with baked blackpudding, stews with sausage, sauerkraut with bacon. On winter Thursday evenings, customers can eat their fill for a set price. About 30 fl. Open daily noon to 11pm.

De Groene Lanteerne (The Green Lantern): 43 Haarlemmerstraat. Tel. 24 19 52. Worth a visit for ambience alone. Claims to be the narrowest restaurant in Europe. 17th century interior. Dutch and French cuisine. About 40 fl.

De Keyzer Bodega: 96 Van Baerlestraat. Tel. 71 14 41. An Amsterdam landmark, across from the Concertgebouw. Cafe tables, with rugs, communal reading table, enclosed terrace. Drinks and/or dinner. Seafood, schnitzels, ranging from 20-40 fl for main dishes. Reservations for dinner essential.

De Nachtwacht (The Nightwatch): 2 Theorbeckeplein. Tel. 22 47 94. Located at the edge of the Rembrandtsplein, on the corner of Reguliersdwarsstraat, this is a famous Amsterdam steak restaurant, crowded on weekday evenings with a well-dressed local set. Shrimp and other seafood, as well as steaks, can be eaten at the active bar and at tables. Starting at about

22 fl, most dishes approximately 30 fl.

d'Vijff Vlieghen (Five Flies): 294 Spuistraat. Entrance at 1 Vlieghendesteeg. Tel. 24 83 69/ 24 52 14. Despite its less than appealing name, this is a world-famous restaurant, extending over five houses, with a number of different rooms, each in its own classic Dutch or Renaissance style. The antiques are gorgeous, and the setting includes original Rembrandt etchings. Originally the site of a 17th-century tavern, the restaurant specializes in French and Dutch cuisine and supplies a wide selection of excellent wines. Unique, and expensive. From 5pm-midnight.

Moeder's Pot Eethuisje: 119 Vinkenstraat. Tel. 23 76 43. Tiny place near the Haarlemmerdijk, which serves huge portions of traditional Dutch chicken, fish and steak dishes. Mugs and pots hanging from the ceiling, a few tables are crammed into the small room. Prices incredibly low for a good solid meal, around 10 fl. A real find.

The Pancake Bakery: 191 Prinsengracht. Tel. 25 13 33. Very near the Anne Frankhuis and a Canal Bike mooring, this is a popular pancake joint for locals and tourists alike. A funky atmosphere with old photos, low beams, sawdust on the floor. Hearty servings. Various kinds for breakfast, lunch, dinner, dessert. Reasonable prices, from about 12 fl.

Seafood

(Note that many steak and Dutch restaurants also serve seafood dishes.)

Bols Taverne: 106 Rozengracht. Tel. 24 57 52. Restored 17th-century warehouse and tasting room for genever and liqueur, transformed into a popular seafood restaurant. Steak and lamb also served. Several rooms, with seafaring decor throughout. Light meals, less expensive, available in the beamed and tiled bar. Main seafood courses from about 30 fl.

Lucius: 247 Spuistraat. Tel. 24 18 31. Casual, congenial, well-known seafood restaurant. Wood-pannelled interior. Carefully prepared fresh catches. Reservations recommended. Main dishes start around 30 fl.

Indonesian

Petit Asli: 33y Waterlooplein. Tel. 26 60 64. Just across the Amstel from the Rembrandtsplein, on the edge of the old Jewish neighborhood, this small restaurant is a pleasant surprise for an Indonesian place. None of the touristy frills, but a simple, pretty setting. The owner/cook scrambles around in a tiny nook of a kitchen behind the counter. She concocts her own dishes, including a nice hot sauce. *Rijsttafels* compare favorably in taste and price to those in larger Indonesian restaurants. Something called the *Nase Rames* is a plate of meats, various vegetables and noodles piled high, for 12.50 fl. Vegetarian dishes as well. Sun.-Thurs., call for hours.

Speciaal: 142 Nieuwe Leliestraat. Tel. 24 97 06. Just outside the main tourist area, this small cozy place serves delicious Indonesian food at reasonable prices, served amid Javanese carpets and bamboo lamps. Reputed by many to be among the best. Popular with locals. Just outside tourist area. *Rijsttafel* for two, around 40 fl.

Indian

Balraj: 1 Binnen Oranjestraat. Tel. 25 14 28. A tiny, simple Indian and Surinamese place near the Haarlemmerdijk, popular with locals. Not elegant, but delicious and inexpensive. A wide variety of Indian dishes, spicy and filling, at low prices. Daily 3-11pm.

Koh-i-noor: 29 Westermarkt. Tel. 23 31 33. It's sister restaurant is *Sher-e-punjab:* 18 Rokin. Tel. 27 21 18. Both these restaurants are near the Dam Square. The first, *Koh-i-noor*, earned a reputation as one of the best Indian restaurants in the city. It is small, lavishly decorated, and always crowded. Reservations highly recommended. *Sher-e-punjab* has a slightly more open and simple decor, but the same menu. Both places provide gracious service and a wide of selection of set menus. These include everything from soup to dessert and a variety of very distinctive sauces and dishes. About 22 fl, and very generous portions. Vegetarian set menu available. Also a wide range of tandoori and curry dishes. One set menu and one separate main dish can probably satisfy two people, if shared. *Sher-e-punjab* is less likely to be full, but offers the same excellence.

Murugan: 192 Rozengracht. Tel. 25 53 76. A little past the Prinsengracht. The setting is intimate and authentically Indian in this small and quiet restaurant, with candles on the table and pleasant service by the owner. A less elaborate menu than the *Koh-i-noor*, but wide and varied nonetheless, with much to choose from for vegetarians. Generous portions. Serving Surinamese food as well. Spicing ranges from subtle to burning hot. Very relaxing, satisfying, pleasant and reasonable.

Vegetarian

Egg Cream: 19 Sint Jacobsstraat. Between the Nieuwezijds Voorburgwal and the Nieuwendijk. A small, homey and popular place, and justifiably so. They make vegetarian eating a joy. Soups are thick and filling. Dinner specials consist usually of a good solid grain dish with side dishes to balance it out. Big slices of delicious fruit pies smothered in fresh cream. You can fill up on fine vegetarian food for 10-15 fl.

Golden Temple Restaurant: 126 Utrechtestraat. Tel. 26 85 60. Peaceful atmosphere, soft music sometimes. Lots of grains. Hefty vegetarian burrito. Run by a spiritual group. About 15 fl.

Manna: 1 Spui. Just off the Kalverstraat, a busy health food store with some table service in their small gallery. Sells delicious and nutritious take-out snacks and ingredients for fast lunches. Various pastries stuffed with soy, vegetables, etc. Great variety and tasty. An economical source for healthy picnic fixings.

Twindekind: 69 Haarlemmerdijk. Tel. 26 87 55. Extremely imaginative and carefully prepared vegetarian cuisine. They use a textured soy product in place of meat which opens all sorts of possibilities for a variety of dishes. Offers something called Japanese pizza. Very careful in selection of organic produce. Delicious vegetarian *sateh*, which with a salad makes a filling meal. About 10 fl. Open 5-9pm daily. Closed Saturday.

Chinese
Treasure Restaurant: 115 Nieuwezijds Voorburgwal. Tel. 23 40 61. Outstanding Chinese dishes including an excellent Peking Duck and a Mongolian Hotspot (by order only). Expensive but highly recommended.

Japanese
Yoichi: 128 Weteringschans. Tel. 22 68 29. Sparsely elegant Japanese decor in a classic two-story Amsterdam setting, complete with steep staircase. Varied menu includes sushi. Service very friendly, very enthusiastic. Crowded with Japanese — the best measure of quality you can find. Some portions large, some traditionally small and concentrated. Dishes cost from 12-60 fl. Ordering several dishes, it is possible to eat a fine and satisfying Japanese meal for about 20-25 fl. A miso soup and Japanese salad will cost less and still satisfy. Reservations recommended.

Mexican
Rose's Cantina: 38 Reguliersdwarsstraat. Tel. 25 97 97. Just about the trendiest place on a street of trendy cafes, bars and restaurants. Jammed nightly, and even more so on weekend nights. But the Mexican food here is tasty, filling and reasonably priced considering the surroundings and clientele. Expect to wait about half an hour. Order a beer and stand at the bar or outside. Singles can order and eat at the bar and avoid the wait. Here you can rub shoulders — literally — with Amsterdam yuppies. Approximately 18-20 fl.

Pasta and Pizza

Burger's Patio: 12 Tuindwarsstraat. Tel. 23 68 54. A combination cafe and restaurant, serving pasta in a hip setting in the heart of the Jordaan district. A favorite with Jordaan locals. Nice tomato soup. A changing menu. Friendly and warm atmosphere. Most pasta dishes from approximately 17.50 fl.

Pizzeria Collina: 145 Rozenstraat. Tel. 25 67 15. Intimate, popular, crowded, not far from the Jordaan, serving pasta and shrimp as well. From 9 fl.

Jewish

Jewish Historical Museum Coffee Shop: 2-4 Jonas Daniel Meijerplein. Tel. 26 99 45. Serving pastries, refreshments, sandwiches, light meals. Dairy. Delicious Sephardic ginger pastries.

Restaurant Swart: 87 Willemsparkweg. Tel. 76 07 00. Traditional Jewish dishes. Specialities include gefilte fish, matzo-ball soup, and Sephardic fish dishes. Not under rabbinical supervision.

Mixed Bag

Le Salut: 287 Prinsengracht. Tel. 27 13 54. This small restaurant serves mainly French dishes, and has a steady, loyal following, as well as a sumptuous, unlimited salad bar (included in the meal). From about 22 fl. Open daily noon-10pm, reservations accepted.

Rias Atlas: 25 Westermarkt. Right next to the *Koh-i noor*, across from Westerkerk. Spanish. Popular and crowded. Wide selection of grilled meats and seafood dishes. Set meals available. From about 20 fl for a satisfying grill plate or seafood dish, with trimmings. A very good stop.

Rum Runners: 277 Prinsengracht. Tel. 27 40 79. Very cool, chic, trendy, in a wide-open, light-filled Caribbean setting filled with tropical plants, and in the middle is an aviary, so the place is filled with the gentle background music of birdsong. Dishes also tend to be exotic, with tropical fruit. Bar as well as sit-down service, patio and gallery. Wear your safari jacket. From about 20 fl. Live music Mondays and Wednesday.

Cafes

There are hundreds of cafes and bars in Amsterdam. Part of exploring the city is discovering your own special little cafe that seems to fit you perfectly. Here are some for starters, spanning a wide range of the different personalities that cafes seem to acquire after a while.

Barney's Breakfast Bar: 102 Haarlemmerstraat. A casual place mostly for the young set. A coffee shop which also serves solid and reasonably priced food. There are also magazines, chess, and an alternative menu. Friendly and relaxed.

Cafe Americain: American Hotel, 97 Leidsekade. Tel. 24 53 22. A classic and famous Amsterdam gathering point right on the edge of the Leidseplein, at which to see and be seen on the patio on pleasant days, or to hang out inside until the wee hours. Both the hotel and its cafe are registered national monuments. Built in the Art Nouveau style of the turn-of-the-century, the cafe has tiled arches, leaded windows, sculptures and carvings. A full meal, about 40 fl.

Cafe Gollem: 4 Raamsteeg (between Spuistraat and the Singel). Tel. 26 66 45. Another popular local drinking hole, known for its selection of some 200 international beers.

Cafe Kalkhoven: Prinsengracht and Westermarkt. One of the oldest in the city, dating to 1670. A beautiful antique interior.

Cafe Schiller: 26 Rembrandtsplein. An Art-Deco gem, and an artists' and literary hang-out in the 20s and 30s, it stands out among the many places on the Rembrandtsplein.

Gambit: 20 Bloemgracht. A small cafe in the Jordaan for chess lovers.

Melkweg Cafe: 407 Marnixstraat. Part of the multi-faceted media maze that is the Melkweg, but with its own entrance until evening, when it is reached through the main entrance where there is admission (see 'The Leidseplein').

Papeneiland: 2 Prinsengracht. Another very famous oldie, one of the many around the Jordaan area.

O'Henry's: 89 Rokin. An English pub, popular with English tourists.

Shaffy: 324 Keizersgracht. A cafe is attached to this progressive theater.

The Old Bell: 46 Rembrandtsplein. Tel. 24 16 28. Near Cafe Schiller. Polished, burnished, cushioned within, an English-style pub, seemingly apart from the square.

The World According to Garp: Reguliersdwarsstraat. Trendy; with a spacious California touch. Music on Sunday.

Entertainment

Live Music, Clubs, Discos

Amsterdam has an eventful and varied live music scene. There is a constant flow of music, out on the streets and in the bars and small cafes. Much of the music is played in the intimate and informal venue of small neighborhood bars. Walking around the Rembrandtsplein or Leidseplein on a weekend night, it might seem that every other bar or restaurant has its own band blaring away. There is some very good jazz, as well as African and Latin beat. And, not suprisingly, the newest in rock and punk finds a showcase here.

For young people, the multimedia centers are some of the best places to hear new and good music, and if you don't like it there is always something else going on anyway. At a more subdued pace, many of those deep-dark brown cafes have a piano and base in the corner striking up something soft and mellow.

Bimhuis: 73-77 Oude Schans. Tel. 23 33 73. Along an old canal warehouse strip, featuring international jazz talent. Wed.-Sat. Workshops as well.

Canecao: 70 Lange Leidsedwarsstraat. Live Brazilian and South American music till the morning in this hideaway off the Leidseplein.

Costes: 9 Rosmarijnsteeg. Japanese jazz in a small cafe.

De Engelbewaarder: 59 Kloveniersburgwal. Tel. 25 37 72. Pleasant and friendly. Sat. and Sun. evening jazz.

De IJsbreker: 23 Weesperzijde. Tel. 93 90 93 (info. only in Dutch). The cafe has a long history as a billiards center, a socialist focal point, a meeting spot for Jewish artists and locals. The vaulted interior has retained its elegance, and the cafe has once again become a cultural center, presenting workshops, lectures, modern innovative music and a wide range of cultural events. Brunch on Sundays, 10am-3pm.

De Kroeg: 163 Lijnbaansgracht. Tel. 25 01 77. Varied repertoire: salsa, reggae, African, blues, Tex-Mex. Starts hopping around 11pm.

De Melkweg: 234 Lijnbaansgracht. Tel. 24 17 77. Constant schedule of concerts, from the whole range of pop and rock,

A night out in a pub

and a recent infusion of ethnic music. Concerts are only part of the cultural extravaganza (see Leidseplein).

Jazzcafe Alto: 115 Korte Leidsedwarsstraat. Tel. 26 32 49. Amsterdam's oldest jazz club swings till 4am every morning with live jazz.

Joseph Lam Jazzclub: 8 Van Diemenstraat. Tel. 22 80 86. Swings to live Dixieland every weekend.

Odeon: 460 Singel. Perhaps the most popular disco in the city. Also a schedule of latenight concerts starting after midnight.

The String: 98 Nes. Tel. 25 90 15. Folk and country music, all week.

Classical Music

Concertgebouw: 98 Van Baerlestraat. Tel. 71 83 45. Ongoing schedule of top classical performers and orchestras. Free concerts every Wed. at 12:30pm.

Nieuwe Kerk: The Dam. Tel. 23 64 32. Organ concerts.

Oude Kerk: 23 Oudekerksplein. Tel. 24 91 83. Organ concerts.

Westerkerk: 281 Prinsengracht. Tel. 24 77 66. Organ concerts.

A MSTERDAM

Filling the Basket: Where to Shop for What

Amsterdam has an abundance of shopping opportunities. It has maintained its traditional position as a major trade center. In addition, there are the products and crafts that Holland is well-known for — cheeses, flowers and bulbs, wooden clogs, furniture, diamonds, Delftware and other china, and chocolates.

Amsterdam has some major department stores, but not many. The best places for shopping are the small shops that are scattered everywhere.

The extended pedestrian mall of the Nieuwendijk/Kalverstraat is one of the main shopping areas in the city. The stores here are big and bright, with the latest styles in vogue. The parallel streets of the Damrak and Rokin are lined with the same kinds of stores, as is the Leidsestraat leading to the Leidseplein. Along these streets can be found large bookstores, electronic and camera stores and clothing boutiques. The two malls are lined with shoe stores. Several of Amsterdam's main department stores are found around the Kalverstraat and Dam Square. Along the Leidseplein many airline offices can also be found, as well as a selection of quaint and charming food stores.

Outside of the main tourist area, there are shopping and browsing strips along Van Baerlestraat, beyond the Museumplein; along Ferdinand Bolstraat around the Albert Cuypmarkt and beyond; and further south along Beethovenstraat. Mainly small shops line these streets, with varying degrees of diversity, charm and class. There is an unusual collection of bookshops, junk shops, etc. along Haarlemmerstraat and along Haarlemmerdijk, west of the Stationsplein. Three adjacent parallel streets intersecting the Prinsengracht — Runstraat, Berenstraat and Reestraat — have clusters of small and unusual shops. Nieuwe Spiegelstraat, heading toward the Museumplein, is lined with some incredible antique stores. These are open late on Thursdays until 9pm.

Amsterdam continues to be a reliable supplier of the goods from its former colonies: spices, coffees, teas, tobacco. Each can be found in specialty shops tucked into corners and sidestreets throughout the city.

*A**MSTERDAM*

Complete listings of stores selling everything from beads to carpets can be found in *Amsterdam This Week*, available around the city.

Amsterdam is considered one of the world centers of the diamond industry, and has been active in diamond production and marketing for 400 years. Craftsmen here became well-known for the precision and quality of their work, and the term 'Amsterdam Cut' is synonymous with quality cutting. The biggest diamond in the world was cut in Amsterdam, as was the smallest.

By 1920, more than 10,000 workers were employed in the diamond industry, with diamond factories throughout the city. The Depression decimated the industry, and World War II devastated the ranks of Jewish diamond workers. It was only some time after the war that the industry began to recover. Businesses which had been scattered through the city moved to central locations accessible to tourists and now offer tours and exhibits. Visitors can watch craftsmen at work, and can learn the meaning of color, clarity, cut, caratage, etc.

Two of the best-known **diamond centers**:
A. van Moppes & Zoon: 2-6 Albert Cuypstraat. Tel. 76 12 42. (Tours Mon.-Sat. 9am-5pm, Sun. 10am-5pm.)

Amsterdam Diamond Center: 1-5 Rokin/29-31 Dam. Tel. 24 57 87. (Open 10am-6pm. Tours 10:30am and 2pm.)

Markets are an indivisible part of Amsterdam and may vary from birds to stamps to cheese. Various markets are referred to in the sections of this book dealing with walks around the city. The area they are part of, and referred to in this book, are listed in parentheses.

Albert Cuypmarkt: Open Mon.-Sat. 9am-5pm. (see 'The Museumplein').

Art Market: Theorbeckeplein, Open April-October Sundays noon-6pm. (see 'The Rembrandtsplein').

Nieuwmarkt: Open Sun., May-Sept. (see 'East of the Dam').

Birds: Noordermarkt at Noorderkerk. Open Saturday morning. (see 'The Jordaan').

Books: Oudemanhuispoort. Open Mon.-Fri. 11am-4pm. (see 'East of the Dam').

Flea Markets: Waterlooplein. Open Mon.-Sat. (see 'The Jewish Quarter'). Noordermarkt, Open Mon. morning (see 'The Jordaan').

Flower Market: On Singelgracht. Open Mon.-Sat. (see 'The Leidseplein').

Stamps and Coins: Nieuwezijds Voorburgwal (near Spui). Open all day Wednesday, and Sat. from 1pm.

Nightshops

Most stores in the city are sealed up from Saturday's closing time to Monday morning. Certain stores, nightshops, will stay open late and on Sundays. They can come in handy but prices can be considerably higher than in a regular grocery store. During the week, most stay open from 4pm-1am, and on Sundays from 11am-6pm. These stores are scattered throughout the city, with two of the more central ones being at 4 Linnaeusstraat and 241 Waterlooplein.

Mouwes Kosher Delicatessen, though not a nightshop, is also open on Sundays, 73 Utrechtsestraat.

At every hour of the day and night, in every season, the canals

Festivals

Amsterdam is a city that knows how to enjoy itself. There is always something going on, somewhere. And for each organized event, there are spontaneous ones popping up suddenly around the city.

February/March	Amsterdam Art Weeks, many special theater performances and exhibitions.
February/March	*Oude Kunst in de Nieuwe Kerk*, Art and Antiques Fair.
February/March	Amsterdam Carnival Parade.
March	*Artis staat in bloei*, Flower exhibition in Amsterdam Zoo.
March	*Hiswa*, Amsterdam Boat and Watersports show.
March	Amsterdam BP — car rally.
March-April	Concertgebouw Orchestra's Easter performance.
April-mid October	Illumination of the City and Canals.
April	Head of the River, International rowing event on the Amstel river.
30 April	The Queen's birthday, all kinds of events and free markets.
May	International Marathon Amsterdam.
May-September	Antique Market (Sundays only, Nieuwmarkt).
June-August	Summer Evening Concerts at the Concertgebouw.
June	Open Air Theatre at the Vondelpark with all kinds of performances.
June-August	Organ concerts in the main churches of Amsterdam.
June	Holland Festival, International Cultural Festival with music, dance, theater, etc.
June	*Kunstrai*, Art Fair with more than 35 leading galleries participating.
July/August	Carillon Concerts in the main churches of Amsterdam.
July	Summer Festival, a selection of the smaller Amsterdam theaters take part in producing a variety of theater performances.
September	*Bloemencorso* — includes flower parade from Aalsmeer to Amsterdam.
September	Antique car parade.

September	Jordaan Festival, typical Amsterdam event.
September	*Amsterdam Mode Stad*, top fashion designers show their collections.
September	Amsterdam Jazz Festival in the Meervaart.
October	*Herfsttentoonstelling*, autumn flower show in the Bosmuseum.
November	Arrival Parade for St. Nicolaas (Sinterklaas), patron saint of Amsterdam.

Important Addresses and Phone Numbers

The area code if you are dialing from outside Amsterdam is 020.

Emergencies
Ambulance: Tel. 5 55 55 55.

Police: Tel. 22 22 22.

Medical and Dental emergency: Tel. 66 42 111.

Chemists: Tel. 44 77 39 or Tel. 94 87 09.

Airport information: Tel. 511 04 32.

Charter information: Tel. 511 06 66.

VVV Tourist information: Tel. 26 64 44.

Taxi Central: Tel. 77 77 77.

Auto breakdowns: Tel. 22 44 66.

Transportation information (GVB): Tel. 27 27 27.

Airlines
British Airways: 4 Stadhouderskade. Tel. 85 22 11.

Canadian Pacific Air: 55 Leidsestraat. Tel. 22 44 44.

KLM: 55 Amsterdamseweg, Amstelveen. Tel. 49 91 23.

Quantas: 9 Rokin. Tel. 25 50 15.

SAA: 2 Stadhouderskade. Tel. 16 44 44.

*I*NDEX

*I*NDEX

NOTES

NOTES

NOTES

NOTES

NOTES

NOTES

NOTES

NOTES

NOTES

NOTES

QUESTIONNAIRE

In our efforts to keep up with the pace and pulse of Amsterdam, we kindly ask your cooperation in sharing with us any information which you may have as well as your comments. We would greatly appreciate your completing and returning the following questionnaire. Feel free to add additional pages. A complimentary copy of the next edition will be sent to you should any of your suggestions be included.

Our many thanks!

To: Inbal Travel Information (1983) Ltd.
2 Chen Blvd.
Tel Aviv 64071
Israel

Name: _____

Address: _____

_____

Occupation: _____

Date of visit: _____

_____

Purpose of trip (vacation, business, etc.): _____

_____

Comments / Information: _____

_____

_____

_____

_____

_____

_____

_____

_____

_____

_____

_____

_____

_____

_____

INBAL Travel Information Ltd.
P.O.B. 39090 Tel Aviv
ISRAEL 61390